Identity

KEYWORDS IN TEACHER EDUCATION

Series Editor: Viv Ellis

Taking cultural theorist Raymond Williams's concept as an organizing device, the *Keywords in Teacher Education* series offers short, accessibly written books on the most pressing and challenging ideas in the field.

Teacher education has a high profile in public policy and professional debates given the enduring associations between how teachers are prepared and how well their students do in school. At the same time, research perspectives on the important topics in the field are increasingly polarized with important consequences for the kind of teacher and the qualities of teaching that are most valued. Written by internationally recognized experts, these titles offer analyses both of the historical emergence and the consequences of the different positions in these debates.

Also available in the series:

Expertise, Jessica Gerrard and Jessica Holloway

Forthcoming in the series:

Communities, Ken Zeichner
Quality, Clare Brooks
Disadvantage, Jo Lampert, Jane Wilkinson, Mervi Kaukko and
     Rocío García-Carrión
Knowledge, Steven Puttick, Victoria Elliott and Jenni Ingram

Identity

SARAH STEADMAN

BLOOMSBURY ACADEMIC
LONDON • NEW YORK • OXFORD • NEW DELHI • SYDNEY

BLOOMSBURY ACADEMIC
Bloomsbury Publishing Plc
50 Bedford Square, London, WC1B 3DP, UK
1385 Broadway, New York, NY 10018, USA
29 Earlsfort Terrace, Dublin 2, Ireland

BLOOMSBURY, BLOOMSBURY ACADEMIC and the Diana logo are
trademarks of Bloomsbury Publishing Plc

First published in Great Britain 2023

Cover design by Charlotte James
Cover image © Zoonar GmbH / Alamy Stock Photo

A catalogue record for this book is available from the British Library.

A catalog record for this book is available from the Library of Congress.

ISBN: HB: 978-1-3502-8592-7
PB: 978-1-3502-8591-0
ePDF: 978-1-3502-8593-4
eBook: 978-1-3502-8594-1

Series: Keywords in Teacher Education

Typeset by Newgen KnowledgeWorks Pvt. Ltd., Chennai, India
Printed and bound in Great Britain

To find out more about our authors and books visit www.bloomsbury.com
and sign up for our newsletters.

This book is dedicated to my parents who have always shown me the kind of teacher I want to be

CONTENTS

FIGURES

SERIES EDITOR'S FOREWORD

This series is organized by the concept of 'keywords', first elaborated by Welsh cultural theorist Raymond Williams (1976), and books in the series will seek to problematize and unsettle the ostensibly unproblematic and settled vocabulary of teacher education. From Williams's perspective, keywords are words and phrases that occur frequently in speech and writing, allowing conversation to ensue, but that nonetheless reveal profound differences in meaning within and across cultures, politics and histories. In teacher education, such keywords include practice, knowledge, quality and expertise. The analysis of such keywords allows us to trace the evolution of the emergent – and the maintenance of residual – meanings in teacher education discourses and practices. By analysing keywords, therefore, it is possible to elucidate the range of meanings of what Gallie (1955) referred to as 'essentially contested concepts' but in ways that promote a critical, historical understanding of changes in the fields in which they occur.

In the first edition of *Keywords*, Williams included entries on 108 units, ranging from 'Aesthetic' to 'Work'. A second edition followed in 1983, and other writers have subsequently used the concept to expand on Williams's original collection (e.g. Bennett, Grossberg and Morris, 2005; MacCabe, Yanacek and The Keywords Project, 2018) or to apply the concept to specific domains (e.g. A Community of Inquiry, 2018). This series applies it to teacher education. The purpose of the series mirrors that of Williams's original project: to trace ideological differences and social conflicts over time as they relate to the discourses and practices of a field (here, teacher education) by focusing on a selection of the field's high-frequency words. So *Keywords in Teacher Education* is not a multi-volume dictionary.

The kind of analysis required by a focus on keywords goes beyond etymology or historical semantics. By selecting and analysing keywords, Williams argued,

> we find a history and complexity of meanings; conscious changes, or consciously different uses; innovation, obsolescence, specialization, extension, overlap, transfer; or changes which are masked by a nominal continuity so that words which seem to have been there for centuries, with continuous general meanings, have come in fact to express radically different or radically variable, yet sometimes hardly noticed, meanings and implications of meaning. (Williams, 1976: 17)

Given the increasingly strong attention paid to teacher education in education policy and in public debates about education more generally, focusing on keywords in this field is both timely and necessary. Uncovering and unsettling differences and conflicts in the vocabulary of preparing teachers renders the political and social bases underlying policy formation and public discourse more visible and therefore more capable of being acted upon.

Through this organizing device, the *Keywords in Teacher Education* series addresses the most important topics and questions in teacher education currently. It is a series of short books written in a direct and accessible style, each book taking one keyword as its point of departure and closely examining its cultural meanings historically whilst, crucially, identifying the social forces and material consequences of the differences and conflicts in meaning. Written by internationally recognized researchers, each peer-reviewed book offers cutting-edge analysis of the keyword underpinned by a deep knowledge of the available research within the field – and beyond it. One of the aims of the series is to broaden the gaze of teacher education research by engaging more systematically with the relevant humanities and social science literature – to acknowledge, as Williams did, that our understanding is deepened and potential for action strengthened by seeking to understand the social relations between words, texts and the multiple contexts in which their meanings are produced.

Identity has long been a keyword in the humanities and social sciences. More recently, the idea has become significant in early-twenty-first-century political debates ranging from, for example, derogatory references to 'identity politics' to the identitarian movement asserting racial dominance over geographic territory. However long identity has been a keyword, it is clear that what it signifies still matters: its meaning is consequential and plays out in the social forces that shape people's lives at the most fundamental level. In the field of teacher education – especially at the level of policy – it also remains significant even if it is not always named and its meanings are implicit. So, for example, teacher education reforms aligned with a 'standards' or competences perspective often simply assume an uncontested notion of what a teacher is, what a teacher needs to be able to know and do, what a teacher believes or professes in terms of values and even, historically, the personal morality and marital status of those allowed to enter the profession. Only a certain kind of person can become a teacher, and so, from this perspective, the sociocultural identity of the teacher is at stake.

From the perspective of human learning and development, identity is also a keyword, of course, and this is where the word figures more explicitly in teacher education research. Whether from social or cultural-historical psychological perspectives, cognitive anthropological, ethnographic or philosophical, identity as a keyword is associated with becoming, and becoming, far from being a 'limp' or wishy-washy synonym for any kind of change, represents instead the most profound kind of psycho-social change – a fundamental reorientation in relations of the self to the social world and a change in both cognitive architecture and personal trajectory of social participation. So learning to become a teacher is more than just the acquisition of a pre-existing professional toolkit of skills; the identity of 'teacher' is highly significant because it is something that is actively worked on by the person wishing to become one.

In this outstanding contribution to the *Keywords in Teacher Education* series, Sarah Steadman shows how identity figures in the broad landscape of teacher education research. She demonstrates the importance of this contested theoretical concept or keyword in deeply practical ways. Understanding the significance of identity is important when designing curricula for initial/pre-service or early career training and development. Identity is important in considering teacher retention within the profession – as Steadman shows, teachers' own engagement in their professional learning and development is sustained in exercising their agency in working on their identity. If you simply tell a teacher what she is, what her identity is and how that has to play out in the social world of classrooms and schools, there is not much for that teacher to become engrossed in – unless of course the object is simply to please the people doing the telling. Steadman draws on the latest research in a range of fields to show why it remains important to consider identity as a keyword in teacher education and why, crucially, it should remain so.

Viv Ellis
Melbourne, 2022

References

A Community of Inquiry. (2018). *Keywords; for Further Consideration and Particularly Relevant to Academic Life, Especially as It Concerns Disciplines, Inter-Disciplinary Endeavor and Modes of Resistance to the Same.* Princeton: Princeton University Press.

Bennett, T., Grossberg, L. and Morris, M. (2005). *New Keywords.
A Revised Vocabulary of Culture and Society.* Oxford: Blackwell
Publishing.

Gallie, W. B. (1955). Essentially Contested Concepts. *Proceedings of
the Aristotelian Society, 56,* 167–98.

McCabe, C., Yanacek, H., and The Keywords Project. (2018).
Keywords for Today. A 21st Century Vocabulary.
Oxford: Oxford University Press.

Williams, R. (1976). *Keywords: A Vocabulary of Culture and
Society.* London: Fontana.

ACKNOWLEDGEMENTS

In writing a book about the identity of teachers and teacher educators, I am reminded of the many pupils, students, teacher candidates and colleagues who have inspired me during my years as a teacher and teacher educator. It is a privilege to have shared classrooms, staffrooms and lecture halls with you all.

Particular thanks go to Viv Ellis, Christine Harrison, Bethan Marshall and Lizzie Rushton for their continued support and interest in my work. To Kate, thank you for listening and laughing with me and showing me the real joy in feeling that someone in the world knows you well. Special thanks to my family and particularly to Luke, Jess and Jack. Thank you for your unfaltering love, support and patience – you continue to shape my identity every day.

CHAPTER ONE

Identity as a Keyword in Teacher Education

Identity provides a lens through which we can come to understand what it is to be a member of an 'impossible profession' (Freud, 2001). Life as a teacher or teacher educator is always in flux, an ongoing reconciliation of personal beliefs and values in a constantly changing, politically charged professional landscape. In coming to the practice of teaching (as a teacher or as a teacher educator), the individual brings the sediments of past experiences, learning and emotions to bear on the localized context, reframing and reconfiguring the self in relation to others in practice that is inevitably contentious (Holland and Lave, 2001). As Alsup (2019) notes,

> The situated identity is always in dialogue with external demands and contexts, as well as with other internal subjectivities, memories, and experiences. It is a continual balance between (and among) self and other. (Alsup, 2019: 131)

Such conflicts and reworkings will be explored in the following pages as we consider the 'shaping and reshaping' (Williams, 1976: 24) of identity in the field of teacher education.

Key Points

- Definitions of identity and the rise in identity politics;
- the relevance of identity as a key word in teacher education;
- the changing nature of professionalism in teaching and its impact on identity.

Identity and Identity Politics

Identity is a complex and slippery term, with meanings ranging from 'absolute or essential sameness; oneness' to 'personal or individual existence' (OED, 2021). Gee (2000) describes identity as pertaining to a 'kind of person' within a particular context and this emphasis on context is central to discussions of identity. In essence, identity cannot be seen in fixed terms. It is not an attribute that someone has, but a changing and developing phenomenon, formed in relation to other people, contexts and experiences. People inhabit multiple identities simultaneously, often spanning the personal and the professional ('mother,' 'friend,' 'lover,' 'teacher,' 'mentor' etc.).

Exploration of identity as a concept has changed over time, from definitions rooted in psychoanalysis (Freud, 1937) to social psychology (Erickson, 1959; Vygotsky, 1978) and anthropology (Holland et al., 1998). Overall, there has been a movement in understandings of identity from a focus on individuality to a more fluid conception that acknowledges change in response to differing social contexts and how characteristics such as race, gender, ethnicity and class can contribute to the formation of cultural identity (Collier and Thomas, 1988; Bourdieu, 1991).

Identity Politics

Identity matters. In recent years, there has been a dramatic rise in so-called identity politics in mainstream politics. The term 'identity politics' was first used in print by Barbara Smith and the Combahee River Collective in their statement published in 1977. Identifying as Black feminists, the Collective's desire for everyone to be 'recognized as human, levelly human' is evident in their assertion that 'the most profound and potentially most radical politics come directly out of our own identity' (Combahee River Collective, 1977: 16). Stemming from a belief that their experiences as Black women differed fundamentally from those of white women, the Combahee River Collective highlight the urgency of understanding and addressing simultaneous factors of oppression such as race, sex and class. As Garza (2019) states, 'Far from being an edict of political correctness, identity politics asks us to see the world as it actually is, and more than that, it demands that we equalize the playing field.'

Oliver (2018) claims the term identity politics is now often 'painfully, and badly, used' particularly by politicians who speak as though having an identity is optional. He cites the former Liberal Democrat leader Tim Farron, who described identity politics to an audience at the Oxford Union as 'poison', 'insidious, irrational, and leading to decisions that threaten our liberty'. Similarly, addressing a conference on the future of the UK in 2018, then environment minister and Brexit advocate Michael Gove spoke of the growing number of people in the Western world looking at political questions through 'the prism of identity', invoking the politics of identity as a threat to the rights of the individual:

> The identitarians want to move away from liberal principles of equal treatment for all, colour-blindness and respect for individual rights. Instead, they embrace a politics which ... demands that people define themselves by their group

membership rather than as autonomous individuals. (Gove, 2018)

This traditional right-wing association with individualism was countered by the emergence in America of a collective right-wing identity centred on whiteness. In their book *Identity Crisis* exploring the 2016 presidential campaign, Sides, Tesler and Vavreck (2018: 87) describe how Donald Trump's primary campaign 'became a vehicle for a different kind of identity politics – oriented around white Americans' feelings of marginalization in an increasingly diverse America.' The 'us against them' rhetoric of Trump's electoral campaign and presidency saw a presentation of white Americans as a discriminated against, endangered group, a feature of what Amy Chua defines as right-wing political tribalism. In her book *Political Tribes*, Chua notes the inevitability of identity politics on both sides of the political spectrum:

> When groups feel mistreated and disrespected, they close ranks and become more insular, more defensive, more punitive, more us-versus-them … Of course, one group's claims to feeling threatened and voiceless are often met by another group's derision because it discounts their own feelings of persecution – but such is political tribalism. Chua (2018: 8–9)

This identity polarization is evident in many aspects of modern populist politics, from the legitimizing of white national groups in America to the nationalistic rhetoric characterizing the Brexit campaign in the UK. Identity politics has its critiques, often rooted in the term's generalized use, as claimed by Kirabo (2018): 'The phrase "identity politics" is merely a pejorative blanket term that invokes a variety of ambiguous, cherry-picked ideas of political failings.' However defined, the undeniable rise of identity politics in recent years serves to illustrate the contemporary relevance of the concept of identity, with debates around definition and usage highlighting its contested and often controversial nature. It is a defining keyword of modern society.

Identity as a Keyword

In explaining the title choice for his book *Keywords: A Vocabulary of Culture and Society*, Raymond Williams comments,

> I called these words Keywords in two connected senses: they are significant, binding words in certain activities and their interpretation; they are significant, indicative words in certain forms of thought. (Williams, 1976: 15)

Identity as a keyword is both 'binding' and 'significant', impacting both our thoughts and actions. Asad Haider, whose book *Mistaken Identity* addresses issues of race and class in the Trump presidency, highlights the interplay between this sense of self and our connections with the world, informed by our personal history: 'Identity is not your essence or what's inside you or at the foundation of you, but it's about all the movement that has led to putting you where you are' (Kumar, 2018). Defining identity inevitably combines discourses of the self and of society as identities are formed through personal reflection and societal interaction. The rise in identity politics emphasizes the influence of group identity, encouraging the definition of the self as synonymous with membership of specific groups. As we will see, such groupings are problematic in the field of teacher education, which encompasses a diverse range of individuals with differing experiences, beliefs and models of expertise.

The varied discourses of identity that address the individual, social, personal and political have rendered identity a 'contemporary buzzword' (Clarke, 2009: 185) in the field of teacher education, with research rooted both in the singular experiences of individuals and the broader societal contexts in which they work. The rapidly expanding identity literature covers multiple contexts and subjects, with explorations of professional and personal identity considered alongside issues of conflict and transition. Many authors adopt a narrative approach to the analysis of identity formation while others foreground the role of emotion in shaping professional learning. Encapsulating both the personal and the professional, identity is historically and culturally constructed and reconstructed over time and in relations with others. At the same time, the situated practice of teaching is enacted in broader political and economic contexts, often characterized by struggle and conflict. As Sachs (2003) outlines,

> Teacher identity stands at the core of the teaching profession. It provides a framework for teachers to construct their own ideas of 'how to be', 'how to act' and 'how to understand' their work and their place in society. (Sachs, 2003: 135)

Engaging in focused identity work with pre-service and in-service teachers is both a necessary aspect of the role of teacher educators and an essential part of their own professional learning and growth.

Addressing the significance of identity to the teaching world in a short book is a challenge. Oliver (2018) claims that 'all politics involves an element of identity' and the same could be said for education. As Wenger (1998) states,

> Education in its deepest sense and at whatever age it takes place, concerns the opening up of identities – exploring new ways of being that lie beyond our current state ... Education is not merely formative – it is transformative ... issues of education should be addressed first and foremost in terms of identities and modes of belonging and only secondarily in terms of skills and information. (Wenger, 1998: 263)

Historically, there are differing conceptions of what constitutes effective teaching and teacher education, with the inevitable 'avalanche of uncertainty' (Britzman, 2009) characterizing formal education foregrounding issues of identity for teachers and teacher educators globally. Teacher and teacher educator identities have been the subject of numerous international reviews (e.g. Beijaard, Meijer and Verloop, 2004; Beauchamp and Thomas, 2009; Izadinia, 2013, 2014), while studies from differing international contexts specifically address issues of teacher educator identity (e.g. Lunenberg, Dengerink and Korthagen, 2014; Posti-Ahokas et al., 2021). Professional identity is often presented as temporal and dynamic, with teachers internally negotiating their personal sense of self alongside the more visible demands of life as a teacher (Alsup, 2019). Akkerman and Meijer (2011: 315) emphasize the transitory nature of the teacher identity, describing the continuous and social nature of identity formation as 'an ongoing process of negotiating and interrelating multiple I-positions.' The extent to which identity is shaped by participation and interaction in educational communities of practice (Wenger, 1998) is another prominent theme in the extensive literature.

Professionalism and Identity

Much of the literature on identity in teacher education focuses on the development of a professional identity. Professionalism is itself a keyword in education, open to individual interpretation that complicates its definition. On the surface, it pertains to the attributes and qualities that are associated with those who are trained and skilled at a professional role, such as teaching. But the nature of professionalism in education (and even whether teaching is a profession) is contested. For example, Evetts (2008) points to a threefold categorization that understands professionalism in terms of an occupational value: an ideology, and a discourse of occupational change and managerial control. Hargreaves (2000) presents a four-stage model. Here, teacher professionalism is presented as passing through four historical phases: the pre-professional age, the age of the autonomous professional, the age of the collegial professional and, finally, the post-professional or postmodern stage characterized by conditions of increasing moral uncertainty for teachers as they deal with a more 'diverse and complex clientele' (Hargreaves, 2000: 175). The extent to which concepts of what it means to be and act as a professional in teaching speaks directly to issues of identity.

Hoyle (1975) first introduced the term 'professionality', distinguishing between a collective *professionalism* relating to issues of status and professional culture and the individualized *professionality* in teachers' professional lives, evident in the definition of professionality offered by Evans (2002):

> an ideologically-, attitudinally-, intellectually- and epistemologically-based stance on the part of an individual, in relation to the practice of the profession to which s/he belongs, and which influences her/his professional practice. (Evans, 2002: 6–7)

To this end, the enactment of professionality is bound up with notions of the self and what it means to be a teacher. Hoyle hypothesized two models of professionality in education, identified as 'restricted' and 'extended' (Hoyle, 1975: 318). The extremes of this professionality continuum are helpfully described by Evans (2008):

> at one end, a model of the 'restricted' professional, who is essentially reliant upon experience and intuition and is guided by a narrow, classroom-based perspective which values that which is related to the day-to-day practicalities of teaching. The characteristics of the model of 'extended' professionality, at the other end of the continuum, reflect: a much wider vision of what education involves, valuing of the theory underpinning pedagogy, and the adoption of a generally intellectual and rationally-based approach to the job. (Evans, 2008: 26)

The extent to which teachers (or teacher educators) can adopt a restricted or extended approach to their professional identity is bound up with issues of educational policy and practice. Sachs (2016) argues that discourses of professionalism are inevitably shaped by the environments in which professionals work, with factors such as the prevalence of performance cultures, increased accountability and teacher standards impacting directly on teacher professionalism. Increased focus on an administrative agenda centred on control and compliance will lead to the creation of a teaching profession whose identity is both limited and prescribed. This echoes Ball (2003), who claims that the prevalence of performativity erodes the identity of teachers:

> The novelty of this epidemic of reform is that it does not simply change what people, as educators, scholars and researchers do, it changes who they are. (Ball, 2003: 215)

The postmodern age identified by Hargreaves has been characterized by 'assaults on professionalism in universities, medicine, teaching and elsewhere' (Hargreaves, 2000: 168), with market principles focused on economic efficiency rather than professional autonomy. Professional development for teachers has increasingly been directed towards narrow, economistic measures of teaching quality (Ellis, Mansell and Steadman, 2021), characterized by compliance and fundamentally impacting on personal and professional identity. Professional autonomy is undermined, leading to teachers who are 'timid in their judgements, whose skills are reduced and whose perception in the community is that of technical worker' (Sachs, 2016: 417). It is this contentious professional landscape that characterizes the development of the teachers' professional identities, as they cope with external pressures and bureaucracy alongside the intensification of their work (Flores, 2020). The 'enduring struggles' (Holland and Lave, 2001) come to bear in the local contentious practice of teaching, enacted against a backdrop of policy intervention.

A Sociocultural Approach

The teacher identity is simultaneously individually constructed and socially negotiated. Social psychologist George Herbert Mead fused the concepts of identity with that of the self, advocating that it is through our communications with others that we learn and adapt:

> The behaviour of an individual can be understood only in terms of the behaviour of the whole social group of which he is a member, since his individual acts are involved in larger, social acts which go beyond himself and which implicate the other members of the group. (Mead, 2015: 6–7)

This sociocultural perspective that embraces notions of becoming permeates this book, further informed by the social practice theorizing of Holland and Lave (2001). They link identity and practice, viewing the individual as 'spread' over the social environment, 'becoming in substance a collection point of socially situated and culturally interpreted experience' (Holland and Lave, 2001: 19). Through the concept of 'history-in-person', identity is presented as combining personal sense-making with participation in local contentious practice:

> One's history-in-person is the sediment from past experiences upon which one improvises using the cultural resources available, in response to the subject positions afforded one in the present. (Holland et al., 1998: 18)

History-in-person combines with broader institutionalized tensions or 'enduring struggles' to impact on local (or situated) contentious practice, reminding us that people are unfinished and identities are always in process, formed and re-formed as we encounter struggles in particular times and places. This is of direct relevance to the identity formation of teachers and teacher educators. The situated practice of education is inevitably filtered through a broader political and economic context, replete with struggle and conflict.

Teaching is unlike other professions in that it is 'always done at the dangerous intersection of personal and public life' (Palmer, 1998: 17). It is intrinsically linked to a sense of self and despite a lack of consensus in the literature as to what identity means in teacher education, there is agreement that the formation of a teacher identity is a key aspect of becoming a teacher (see e.g. Flores and Day, 2006; Izadinia, 2013; Nguyen and Loughland, 2017). There are many ambiguities related to the development of teacher educator identity (Izadinia, 2014), but explorations of professional identity are frequently combined with considerations of identity shifts and boundary crossing, noting how the '"kind of person" one is recognized as "being" … can change from context to context, and, of course, can be ambiguous or unstable' (Gee, 2000: 99). Identity is, therefore, both an important and contested concept in the teacher education field.

About the Book

This book explores the tricky concept of identity in the world of teacher education. It is impossible to simplify the beliefs and practices of teacher educators into a homogeneous group, and an attempt to do so would fail to acknowledge the various challenges that are present across contexts. University and school-based teacher educators are joined by others based in communities, many of whom may not even identify themselves as educators at all (Ducharme, 1993; White, 2019). The work of teacher educators varies within and between contexts, often necessitating the simultaneous management of multiple professional roles. Unpacking the messy and recursive process of becoming a teacher or a teacher educator is important, foregrounding the personal and the professional aspects of identity. How these two elements intersect and interact to inform practice is the focus of this book, highlighting the relevance of context and policy in shaping the work of teacher educators.

This exploration of identity as a keyword in the world of teacher education begins with the individual. Chapters 2 and 3 address the identity formation of teachers and teacher educators, exploring what professional identity looks like in the education field. Rooted in an understanding that the complexity and fluidity of becoming a teacher informs the work of teacher educators, Chapter 2, 'Identity and Becoming a Teacher', addresses the concept of what it means to be a teacher, with a particular focus on the process of learning to teach. Issues of identity and agency are considered alongside exploration of the nature of professionalism and the limitations on the developing professional identity of teachers. Chapter 3, 'The Identity of Teacher Educators', specifically addresses the professional identity of this often ambiguous and variously perceived heterogeneous group. The difficulties in pinpointing their role and stance across local, national and international contexts is examined, alongside consideration of the transitions that occur as teacher educators move between positions and places.

The multifaceted nature of the teacher educator identity is further complicated by a lack of certainty about exactly what teacher educators should know and do. In Chapter 4, 'Identity in Practice', it is argued that engaging with issues of identity provides a way for teacher educators to participate in and think about the nature of what they do. Acknowledging the presence of multiple identities, this chapter also addresses the intersectional nature of identity and the limited demographic diversity in teacher education. The formation and evolution of identity is not a solitary task and Chapter 5, 'Social Identity and Collaborative Practices', focuses on the development of professional identity in shared contexts. The relevance of sustained collaboration and partnership working is explored, looking at how embracing the contributions of educators in schools, universities and the community at large has the potential to enact a more democratic approach to teacher education (Zeichner, Payne and Brayko, 2015; Payne and Zeichner, 2017), inviting reconceptualization of the role and identity of teacher educators. In Chapter 6, 'Identity, Conflict and Innovation', tensions in the formation of the teacher educator identity are addressed, considering how the ongoing de-professionalization of teacher educators by restrictive educational policy undermines professional identity and autonomy. The changing nature of professional identity in the digital world is addressed, including the impact of the Covid-19 pandemic on the identity of teacher educators. The book concludes by returning to the significance of identity as a keyword in teacher education and consideration of the nature of the research that characterizes identity work in the field.

CHAPTER TWO

Identity and Becoming a Teacher

Teaching is complex, and research into how teachers think and work is both extensive and inconclusive. However, it is widely asserted that the formation of the teacher identity is an integral part of the process of learning to teach (Beijaard, Meijer, and Verloop, 2004; Alsup, 2006; Beauchamp and Thomas, 2009), with the emerging identity of newcomers to the profession framed around such questions as 'Who am I as a teacher?' and 'What kind of teacher do I want to become?' (Beijaard and Meijer, 2017: 177). As such, this chapter addresses issues of teacher identity, with a particular focus on the process of learning to teach. The increasing diversity in teacher preparation and the varied early career experience of teachers accentuates the centrality of the teacher educator role in guiding and leading developing teachers through times of change.

Key Points

- The relationship between teacher learning and identity and how the development of a teacher identity is impacted by the various cultural myths (Britzman, 2003) that inform personal and societal expectations;

- the role of emotions and tensions in shaping teacher identity;

- identity, agency and how engagement with local figured worlds (Holland et al., 1998) can impact identity production in the world of teaching;

- the centrality of context in the formation of the teacher identity.

A Process of Becoming

Because learning transforms who we are and what we can do, it is an experience of identity. It is not just an accumulation of skills and information, but a process of becoming. (Wenger, 1998: 215)

Learning to teach is a complex task, incorporating subject, pedagogical and contextual knowledge. But it also goes beyond these parameters, inviting questions around the motivation to teach, the type of teacher newcomers to the profession want to become and the positioning of teachers in their social and cultural environment. To this end, learning to teach is an 'identity making process' (Beijaard, 2019: 1) in which Wenger's words resonate. Those entering the profession are not just 'being' teachers but are 'becoming' teachers. They are simultaneously learning how to teach while teaching others, inhabiting the oxymoronic state of 'student teacher' (Britzman, 2003) and engaging in individual sense-making. Equally, in-service teachers continue to shape their practice in response to their personal and professional experiences. Learning, and specifically teacher learning, can therefore be conceptualized as identity learning (Geijsel and Meijers, 2005; Beijaard, 2019), drawing on personal aspects, including 'one's own biography, aspirations, learning history, and beliefs about education' (Beijaard, 2019: 3) but enacted in a professional arena and in response to social, cultural and political discourses. The process of learning helps to shape the person, linking learning and identity. As Mockler comments, 'Teacher professional learning has the capacity to constitute one element of "identity work" for teachers, lying at the intersection of professional context and personal experience and requiring both professional and personal relevance to lead to changes in practice' (Mockler, 2013: 42). Teacher identity is often presented in sociocultural terms, with an understanding of learning as a social process and an emphasis on the interaction between developing people and the culture in which they live (Britzman, 2003; Buchanan and Olsen, 2018). While there are varied conceptions of teacher identity in the vast literature, there is broad agreement that teacher identities are multiple and fluid (Beijaard, Meijer and Verloop, 2004; Flores and Day, 2006; Sachs, 2005) and always impacted by physical, social and political contexts (Connelly and Clandinin, 1999). Teaching is both a personal and professional endeavour and trying to balance the two is part of the process of becoming a teacher (Nias, 1986, 1996; Alsup, 2006; Pillen, Beijaard and den Brok, 2013; Olsen, 2016). Useful categorizations of the nature of teacher professional identity in the existing literature are provided by Olsen (2012), whose review reveals a 'loose, tacit, consensus' that teacher professional identity is:

1. dynamic, and not fixed;
2. both a process and a product;
3. an ongoing and situated relationship among person, others, history and professional contexts;
4. a political project as much as a philosophical frame;
5. socially situated and therefore not traditionally psychological;
6. clearly differentiated from a teacher's 'role'; and
7. not clearly differentiated from a teacher's 'self'.

(Olsen, 2012: 1123)

The classroom is not unfamiliar territory, but beliefs and values are challenged and reworked as personal experiences of school are revisited from the other side of the metaphorical teacher's desk. Accounts of pre-service teacher identity development frequently reference duality and balancing (Steadman, 2021) as the boundaries between the personal and the professional are negotiated. The complex transition from student to teacher is emotional and replete with tensions (Pillen, Beijaard and den Brok, 2013). There is also a close relationship between teacher identity and continuing professional development, prompting studies drawing on identity as a lens for the analysis of teacher learning (Brunetti and Marston, 2018).

Developing a Teacher Identity

Becoming a teacher begins long before taking the active step to train, with views of teachers and teaching informed by individual experiences of classrooms and schools. In *Schoolteacher*, his sociological study of teaching, Lortie coined the term 'apprenticeship of observation' commenting that, 'the average student has spent 13,000 hours in direct contact with classroom teachers by the time he [sic] graduates from high school.' (Lortie, 1975: 61). He suggests that notions of what constitutes a 'good' or 'bad' teacher are informed by the past experience of encounters with particular teachers and kinds of teaching. It is certainly common in research to hear stories of how pre-service teachers have formed ideas of teachers and teaching from their own inspirational teachers. In this extract from research conducted with pre-service secondary English teachers in England, participant Peter describes the influence of his English teacher: 'She had a real passion for English. You could really tell. Her lessons – even if we were doing drier things – were always interesting, always fast-paced. She just made me – I've had teachers throughout school and even outside of school I always had teachers that I've looked up to and respected' (Steadman, 2020).

Inevitably, experiences are not always so positive. In their exploration of Lortie's work regarding mathematics teaching, Mewborn and Tyminski (2006) quote the description of mathematics classes from their research participant Morgan:

> In middle and high school math classes bored me. I remember sleeping every day in my ninth grade algebra class and still making an A. My teachers just did not make it fun and interesting. All I did was homework that my class went over each day. That is all we did. We never did practical word problems or explored math beyond the walls of the school building. When I took classes like geometry, trigonometry, and calculus I really started hating math. Not only was it boring, but it was also harder and more frustrating. (Mewborn and Tyminski, 2006: 31)

Memorable is not always synonymous with interesting, but in both of the above cases, the memory of past experiences influences the future practice of the teachers. Beliefs and values will inevitably have been formed through years of 'intuitive and imitative' observation (Lortie, 1975: 62).

Citing beliefs as the 'building blocks of a teacher's professional identity,' Beijaard and Meijer (2017: 179) highlight the necessity of exploring pre-service teachers' beliefs before they start teaching. They discuss how views are likely to change as pre-service teachers move into their role as teacher, with previously stable beliefs becoming precarious. Earlier research by Watt, Richardson and Tysvaer (2007) in Australia stemmed from an assertion that the values, beliefs and motivations of pre-service teachers have been too long overlooked. Profiling 500 graduate-level entrants to teacher education programmes on entry (and again at the end of their training), they identified three clusters of beginning teacher types – namely, highly engaged persisters (motivated individuals planning to remain in teaching for the duration of their professional career), highly engaged switchers (motivated individuals who are committed to teaching but plan to leave in the future) and lower engaged desisters (individuals with little motivation to teach and who plan to leave the profession as soon as possible). The differing goals and motivations, they argue, will lead to inevitable differences in the pathways of professional identity and development and invite the question as to whether all teacher education programmes should engage in the systematic profiling of pre-service teachers on entry.

The development of teachers is sometimes presented as a linear pathway, with a progression from novice to expert with the accumulation of practical knowledge, 'the more one teaches, the more proficient one becomes' (Lampert, 2010: 27). However, elsewhere it is recognized that progress from novice to professional is 'very likely to be fragmentary and erratic' (Furlong and Maynard, 1995: 98), reflecting the dynamic and ongoing nature of the construction of professional identity. In her exploration of two novice teachers from different US programmes (Urban Teacher Residency and a university-based teacher programme), Gatti (2016: 54) found the pathway of learning to teach to be 'a non-linear, recursive, and messy process'. In the case of one of her participants, Sam, it was engagement with the relational aspects of teaching that became the catalyst for changes in her understanding as she observed her interactions with students on video. It is not Sam's movement through a series of practised encounters over time that impact on her development, nor her passage through a linear process, but her engagement with the relational aspects of her teaching to centre her own identity as a teacher. Her learning to teach process is inextricably linked to her learning to know her students and developing the confidence to 'make herself be known by and vulnerable with her students' (Gatti, 2016: 78). Similarly, Hong, Day and Green (2018) reference the provisional nature of professional identities in the early years of teaching as teachers become exposed to the various tensions and demands of the work. Managing differing situated contexts is juxtaposed with the navigation of national policy and accountability measures. Their exploration of the tensions related to the formation of teacher identities for pre-service and early career teachers revealed patterns of managing and coping over time that highlight the transitional nature of professional identity.

While there are links between the development of expertise and the formation of the professional identity (Peterman, 2017), representation of the development of expertise beyond the preparation period is conflicting. Earlier studies present expertise as a 'state'. Echoing the linear trajectory, Berliner (1988) views the development of expertise in teaching as a series of five stages of skill development: novice, advanced beginner, competent, proficient and expert. This expert–novice comparison approach is based on a premise that experience equates directly to expertise. In contrast, a sociocultural approach presents teacher knowledge and expertise as situated, highlighting the interaction of the whole person with the setting of activity (Lave and Wenger, 1991). However conceptualized, the years immediately post-qualification can see new teachers struggling with the unpredictability of their role (Saber, 2004; Olsen, 2016), and even experiencing a 'praxis shock' (Veenman, 1984; Smagorinsky et al., 2004):

> The transition from teacher training to the first teaching job could be a dramatic and traumatic one. In the English and German literature this transition is often referred to as the 'reality shock', 'transition shock', 'Praxisschock', or 'Reinwascheffekt'. In general, this concept is used to indicate the collapse of the missionary ideals formed during teacher training by the harsh and rude reality of everyday classroom life. (Veenman, 1984: 143)

The often conflicting environments of the training site and the classroom can be hard for pre-service teachers to reconcile. For the early career teacher, the pressures of managing classrooms combined with the relentless nature of teaching preparation and delivery can lead to feelings of isolation and demoralization. The desire to 'make a difference' is juxtaposed with the challenges of managing the proximal and distal contexts (Hong, Day and Green, 2018) of the education world, further problematizing the development of professional identity.

Images of Teacher Identity

Unpacking what it means to be a teacher also entails working through the societal and cultural presentation of the role. Weber and Mitchell (1995) discuss how personal experience is coupled with preconceptions and images of teachers prevalent in popular culture, informing ideas about what it is to be a teacher. They reference playground chants and songs that demonize teachers. Seen as 'super-human role models' with 'eyes in the back of their heads', cultural references present a view of teachers and teaching that is far removed from the realities of the classroom. Those entering the profession must reconcile past, current and future visions of school: 'Even before children begin school, they have already been exposed to a myriad of images of teachers, classrooms and schools which have made strong and lasting impressions on them' (Weber and Mitchell, 1995: 2).

Such cultural images combine with the 'sediments' (Holland et al., 1998) of past experiences of school to impact on the developing teacher identity. As Geijsel and Meijers (2005: 423–4) remind us, 'Identity is a learning process: it is not something that happens to you, but something that you try to construct with the help of culturally available building materials.'

These 'building materials' are not always helpful to the process of professional identity construction. In *Practice Makes Practice*, her critical study of learning to teach, Deborah Britzman (2003) explores how our universal familiarity with the educational world perpetuates a belief that anyone can teach. Britzman identifies three cultural myths rooted in an individualistic view of education rooted in past experience that undermines the social context of teaching and learning to teach. The first myth, 'everything depends on the teacher', rests on the mutual understanding of teachers and students that the teacher is expected to establish control and that, if they fail, control will be handed to the students. This is isolating and potentially suppressive of the 'student' element of the emerging teacher identity. A lack of focus on learning is at the heart of the second myth that presents the 'teacher as expert', playing to the cultural expectations that teachers will have the answers. Ongoing learning is marginalized, with the expert stance seen as particularly problematic for the student teacher who is both being educated and educating others. Thirdly, in the myth that 'teachers are self-made', personal autonomy takes the place of social relationships and the relevance of theory is replaced by the image of the natural teacher, where pedagogy becomes a cult of personality and is reduced to teaching style alone.

By subscribing to cultural myths, teacher learning is restricted as pre-service teachers struggle to cope with the pressures to embody an authoritative discourse on teaching that sees learning as synonymous with control. In this power struggle, learning is dependent on the teacher establishing order and maintaining the stability of the institution. There is no room for experimentation, and uncertainty is positioned as a 'character flaw' that is not welcome in a profession dependent on expertise and compliance. The constant promotion of individualism in these cultural myths denies the developing teacher the necessary social interaction and engagement with the emotionality of learning to teach. As Britzman (2003: 31) comments, 'Learning to teach is a social process of negotiation rather than an individual problem of behaviour.'

Emotions and Identity

Consideration of the developing teacher identity provides opportunities for reflection on the emotions that teaching elicits. Identity development as a learning process may start with experience but is always coupled with emotion (Meijers and Wardekker, 2003; Geijsel and Meijers, 2005). All prospective teachers have an experience of teachers but not of the emotional journey of becoming a teacher, and learning to teach is inevitably emotionally charged (Burn, Hagger and Mutton, 2015).

Towards the end of his life, Russian psychologist Lev Vygotsky developed the concept of *perezhivanie*, describing how the influence of any environment on a child is filtered through their emotional experience. It is not the presence of factors in an environment that influence development but 'the same factors refracted through the prism of the child's emotional experience [perezhivanie]' (Vygotsky, 1994: 339). This idea accentuates the extent to which learning is influenced both by the capacity to interpret and question social practices and by the emotional reactions to such observations. Emotion and motivation are inextricably linked and impact on the formation of identity in the social environment.

Jennifer Nias's book based on the personal accounts of teachers working in infant, junior and middle schools addresses the emotional reality of classroom practice. Her interviews of approaching hundred teachers in England took place over forty years ago, but the narrated experience of struggle during their first experience of work still resonates. Her analysis juxtaposes the formation of socially regulated teacher 'selves' with the unruly and acutely personal. As she states, 'No account of primary teachers' experience is complete if it does not make room for potentially dangerous emotions such as love, rage, and jealousy, on the one hand, and intermittent narcissism and outbreaks of possessive dependence on the other' (Nias, 1986: 203).

As teachers invest their 'selves' in their work (Nias, 1996), personal and professional identities can merge. Examining the emotional experiences of Chinese pre-service teachers, Deng et al. (2017) found emotions to be dynamic and evolving during the teaching practicums. They chart an emotional trajectory that moves through five stages during the teaching practicum identified by emotional responses: eagerness and anxiety, shock and embarrassment, anger and puzzlement and then helplessness and loneliness towards the end. After the teaching practicum, their participants experienced guilt and regret. Their findings indicate the complexity and the uncertainty of student teachers' professional identity formation and the extent to which teachers 'invest their personal sense of identity in their work'. (Nias, 1989: 224–5). Similarly, Timoštšuk and Ugaste's (2012) work with pre-service teachers at Tallinn University in Estonia revealed the presence of negative emotions, which served to overshadow the more positively felt aspects of the learning to teach experience. While the interaction with pupils engendered largely positive emotion, strong negative emotions were expressed in relation to teachers in both the practice school and university. Feelings such as disappointment and anxiety were found to impact on social learning and directly influence the development of professional identity (Timoštšuk and Ugaste, 2012: 430).

The emotionality of teaching inevitably leads to the presence of tensions. Pillen, Beijaard and den Brok (2013) identified thirteen tensions in the literature pertaining to the development of pre-service teachers' professional identity. In their own research with twenty-four pre-service teachers, they cite the 'top three' as 'Wanting to care for students, versus being expected to be tough', 'Wanting to invest in a private life versus feeling pressured to spend time and energy on work' and 'Experiencing conflicts between one's own and others' orientations regarding learning to teach' (Pillen, Beijaard and den Brok, 2013: 253). The last of these is particularly relevant to the work of teacher educators who work with students undertaking practicums. Pre-service teachers will typically find themselves having to manage different sites of learning, with universities and other teacher education centres working alongside mentors in schools. Some teacher preparation programmes also utilize virtual sites, including online learning platforms. The management of these differing locations can lead to the formation of inner doubts or 'critical conflicts' (Vasilyuk, 1988) that can leave individuals feeling vulnerable as they find themselves caught in the double bind (Bateson et al., 1956) of simultaneously trying to satisfy the demands of their teacher education providers and their placement schools.

Research undertaken in England (Steadman, 2021) revealed a tension for some pre-service teachers between university preparation and the experience they encountered in schools during the practicum. Demonstrated pedagogical models of teaching in the university setting were largely discussion based and interactive, presenting a social constructivist view of English teaching that sat in opposition to some local school practices. The friction is demonstrated by one participant's encounter with local school practices in her first placement that promoted quiet, individualized working:

> The thing is the head of English came into that class and she was like oh I'm really impressed that they're all super quiet. For me – I don't like that at all; I honestly don't. I would rather you talk, you discuss. When I say discuss and they don't say anything I'm just like – I would love it if there's talking going on. Yeah that's what I would prefer, just kind of more conversational as well. (Steadman, 2021: 5)

She experienced a conflict between the beliefs and practices extolled by her university and her school placement; to succeed in the school, she faced a dilemma on an emotional level as she was required to behave in a way that was counter to both her instruction and her emerging identity as a teacher. Similarly, Jóhannsdóttir's (2010: 315) research in Iceland explores the contradictions experienced by pre-service teachers working in classrooms whilst also undertaking an online teacher education learning programme. Experience of a double-bind situation occurred as they grappled with the 'conflict between ideal type of work and reality in practice.'

Teacher Identity and Agency

There is a direct link between identity and agency evident in the literature on identity in teaching (Day et al., 2006; Beauchamp and Thomas, 2009; Beijaard, Meijer, and Verloop, 2004;

Beijaard and Meijer, 2017), with one writer describing the two concepts as 'intertwined' (Buchanan, 2015). Teacher agency is traditionally seen as synonymous with the ability to make active choices, equated with the capacity to identify goals and evaluate success (Taylor, 1977). A helpful definition is provided by Toom, Pyhältö and Rust (2015): 'Teacher agency is defined as willingness and capacity to act according to professional values, beliefs, goals and knowledge in the different contexts and situations that teachers face in their work both in classrooms and outside of them' (Toom, Pyhältö and Rust, 2015: 616).

However, learning to teach takes place in multiple and often conflicting contexts, and pre-service teachers in particular can find themselves externally acquiescing to local practices. This can lead to appropriation, as they 'internalize[s] ways of thinking endemic to specific cultural practices' (Grossman, Smagorinsky and Valencia, 1999: 15), resistance or inertia and feelings of helplessness. Although teacher education has the potential to provide an arena for challenge and reflection on learning and teaching, such critical reflection assumes a capacity to transcend and alter existing practices. This level of agentic energy may not be achievable when pre-service teachers are limited by the navigation of conflicts and contradictions within and between sites or the emotionality of transitioning from one state or place to another. For example, Smagorinsky, Lakly and Johnson's (2002) study of six pre-service teachers from a university cohort over a two-year period highlights how the process of figuring out an identity as a teacher can be hindered by the existence of values and practices that contradict personal views and beliefs. In many ways, the intensity of teacher preparation and the emphasis on completion sits in opposition to ideas of becoming that embrace uncertainty and introspection. Theorizing the concept of professional agency, Edwards (2015) observes how professions are strengthened by collaborative work and the internal and external enactment of values and commitment. School mentors and teacher educators have a pivotal role to play in 'making professional values explicit, connecting beginning teachers with the purposes of education and demonstrating peer expectations of professional commitment' (Edwards, 2015: 784).

Holland et al. (1998) explore the broader links between identity and agency in their conception of figured worlds. Here, identity is presented as being about how people learn to understand themselves, how they 'figure' who they are in the 'worlds' that they inhabit and the interactions that take place within them. This exploration of identity addresses the paradoxical notion of people being both products of social discipline and capable of improvisation. People associate with cultural forms and practices, combining the 'intimate or personal world' with the 'collective space of cultural forms and social relations' (Holland et al., 1998: 5). Within the figured world context, people can direct their own actions, model possibilities and inspire action. Through the figured world's lens, people are actors who can both adhere to or depart from the script of the figured world narrative.

Conceptually, figured worlds are significant to the formation of identity within education environments. Engagement with local figured worlds can impact identity production and can lead to developmental changes. Urrieta (2007) chronicles such a shift in his research conducted with Mexican American urban educators, detailing how they became Chicana/o activists by participating in the figured worlds of Chicana/o activism. The work centred on four groups of self-identified Chicana/o activist educators: undergraduates planning to enter the field of education, K-12 teachers, graduate students in education programmes and professors of education. Using life history and ethnographic interviews alongside classroom observation transcripts and artefacts, Urrieta builds a picture of how participation in local Chicana/o activist figured worlds in college or university had resulted in a 'shifting to a new sense of self.' As Urrieta summarizes,

Thus these local figured worlds were the sites of Chicana/o Activist identity production. These worlds provided for participants identifiable cultural, political, social, and historical landscapes, access to a more enduring identity, and other persons similar to them that they could relate to in the midst of the alienating whitestream university environments they found themselves in. Participants 'figured' themselves out as actors in relation to landscapes of people and action in Chicana/o activist local figured worlds. This meant that participants produced or began to produce identities as Chicana/o Activists by participating in the activities organized in Chicana/o activist figured worlds. (Urrieta, 2007: 124)

The local figured worlds of schools are historical phenomena already familiar to those entering the profession, and the relevance of personal school experience to the development of teachers has been widely documented (see, for example, Flores and Day, 2006). Past experience is brought to bear as previous students enter classrooms as new teachers, refiguring who they are and what values they hold. Equally, as pre-service teachers come to know the typical narratives, actions and outcomes of their schools and teacher preparation sites, they can begin to interpret themselves and their actions in relation to those narratives and values. As Gee (2014) notes, there is nothing static about figured worlds. Ultimately, agency is not a possession, but an expression of what people do (Biesta, Priestley and Robinson, 2015) and its enactment in schools depends on the extent to which individuals can pursue their beliefs and values in an environment impacted by physical, social and political contexts (Connelly and Clandinin, 1999).

Identity in Context

Many studies have centred the importance of context in the formation of the teacher identity (Grossman, 1990; Smagorinsky et al., 2004; Flores and Day, 2006; Olsen, 2016) and how interaction with others in the professional context impacts on the development of a teacher (Sachs, 2005; Flores and Day,

2006). Active membership of a community of professionals in schools will inevitably influence identity development for all staff, although this is likely to be most acutely felt by beginning teachers who may be particularly susceptible to the pressures of both school and wider political contexts. As Beauchamp and Thomas (2009) note, 'It might be expected that new teachers, whose identities are only tentative, will particularly feel the impact of a community context and will need to be aware of the shaping of their own identities that will take place in this context' (Beauchamp and Thomas, 2009: 180).

An emphasis on social participation is central to the theory of community of practice (Wenger, 1998; Lave and Wenger, 1991), a means of examining the learning that happens among practitioners in a social environment. Wenger (1998) emphasizes the interplay between the nature of practice and identity: 'There is a profound connection between identity and practice. Developing a practice identity requires the formation of a community whose members can engage with one another and thus acknowledge each other as participants' (Wenger, 1998: 149).

The communities of practice lens has been adopted by many researchers to analyse the identify formation of teachers. In their Australian study, Nguyen and Loughland (2018) explore the positive impact of pairing pre-service teachers together in school placements. Drawing on Wenger's (2000) theory of identity formation that links identity and learning and foregrounds the role of participation with others in social contexts, they found that the pairings 'facilitated a sense of belonging in terms of engagement, imagination and alignment' (Nguyen and Loughland, 2018: 94). The provision of pairings enabled participants to look beyond the situated practice of the given institution, exploring their shared identities in the schools.

The process of socialization in learning is highlighted by Ó Gallchóir, O'Flaherty and Hinchion (2018) in their research conducted in the Republic of Ireland. Their exploration of meaning-making in the development of seven pre-service teachers on a Teacher Education programme emphasizes the ongoing nature of learning. They pay particular attention to the role of the school placement in enacting identity change as the participants transition from the protected training environment into practice in schools. Their findings point to a preoccupation amongst the participants with their physical presence and how that links to ideas of a 'good' or 'bad' teacher. Having managed to overcome this in their reflections, the pre-service teachers then displayed some 'identity unease or distress' when moving between school placements and their sessions in the university. This was particularly evident in the reflection of two of the participants who struggled to identify as a teacher at all when removed from the environment of the school placement: 'Luke and Evan appear to be contextually splitting the role (identity). This would undoubtedly have ramifications for the pre-service teachers' development if they felt a student identity was enacted on campus rather than a pre-service (student) teacher identity' (Ó Gallchóir, O'Flaherty and Hinchion, 2018: 148).

Ó Gallchóir, O'Flaherty and Hinchion (2018: 152) question the value of 'directing content at student teachers during the on-campus portion of their ITE programmes if the so-called "teacher" portion of their identities is dormant until entering a schooling context'. Similarly, Zeichner and Tabachnik (1981) refer to the 'washout effect' in the United States, whereby content from progressive campus experiences is diluted or removed by the more traditional approach adopted in schools. Despite the age of their review and inevitable changes in terminology over time, the broader issues around the nature of teacher identity in differing spaces are still pertinent (Olsen, 2016).

Conclusion

Issues of identity are central to the formation of a teacher. Prospective teachers are not learning in a vacuum, and encounters with the environment and a changing cast of professionals are pivotal in the construction of the self and the formation of identity. As Holland et al. (1998: 27) observe, 'Socially constructed selves ... are subject to positioning by whatever powerful discourses they happen to encounter.' The discourses of managerialism dominate much of international education policy, requiring a reshaping and recreating of professional identities of pre-service and in-service teachers in relation to restricted contexts. The formation of the teacher identity in the process of learning to teach is further complicated by the presence of conflicting views and practices, with prospective teachers potentially caught in the double bind of trying to satisfy the demands of differing people while striving to reconcile their own beliefs and emotional tensions.

Professional learning and the exploration of identity are inextricably linked. Actively engaging with the cacophony of beliefs, values, myths and preconceptions that characterize the teaching experience can help teachers to reflect on their developing professional identity in an educational world that is often dominated by compliance and control. Although awareness of the complexities and contradictions in the development of the teacher identity is important for the work of teacher educators, use of the 'teacher identity' as a lens for learning is rare (Beijaard and Meijer, 2017). Providing opportunities for ongoing, focused reflection on what it means to be a teacher in an increasingly complex and contested educational landscape is part of the vital identity work of teacher education.

CHAPTER THREE

The Identity of Teacher Educators

Globally, teacher educators form a heterogeneous group, comprising a wide range of experiences and working in contrasting contexts. A focus on identity is a common theme in research irrespective of context, frequently combined with considerations of identity shifts and boundary crossing. This chapter focuses on the professional identity of teacher educators, exploring both why there is so much interest in the notion of identity and how the role of the teacher educator differs across contexts.

Key Points

- Why identity is interesting for researchers in teacher education;
- the challenges in identifying a teacher educator identity and defining the role;
- the differing contexts in which teacher educators work and the transitions encountered as they enter new institutions or cross the boundary between being

teachers themselves and inducting others into the world of teaching;

- the role of professional development for teacher educators as a means of developing professional identity and the lack of coherence across contexts and countries.

Why We Need to Talk about Identity

In 2005, Murray and Male described teacher educators as an 'under-researched and poorly understood occupational group' (Murray and Male, 2005: 125). Since that time, there has certainly been an increased focus on the professional identity and work of teacher educators in research literature. Reviews have highlighted the centrality of the development of a teacher educator identity in becoming a teacher educator (Izadinia, 2014; Lunenberg, Dengerink and Korthagen; 2014), and many studies have considered the characteristics of professional teacher educators and the enactment of their identity (Murray, Czerniawski and Barber, 2011; Loughran and Menter, 2019). Attention has been given both to the identity development of beginning teacher educators (Amott, 2018; Hamilton, 2018) and to the ongoing development of experienced educators (Griffiths, Thompson and Hryniewicz, 2014; Hiralaal, 2018). Research has considered the identity of teacher educators in university contexts (Dinkelman, 2011; Tryggvason, 2012), schools (White, 2013; Uibu et al., 2017) and collaborative settings (Waitoller and Kozleski, 2013; Zeichner et al., 2016). Elsewhere, focus has fallen on the professional learning of teacher educators (Meeus, Cools and Placklé, 2018; Czerniawski et al., 2018). Recently, studies have addressed the impact of the Covid-19 pandemic on the identity and professional lives of teacher educators (Darling-Hammond and Hyler, 2020; Ellis, Steadman and Mao, 2020).

The plethora of research invites questions as to why the identity of the teacher educator is so interesting to so many researchers. Part of the answer to this lies in the self-reflexive nature of much of the research. As noted by Zeichner (1999: 8), 'The birth of the self-study in the teacher education movement around 1990 has been probably the single most significant development ever in the field of teacher education research.' The dominance of studies conducted by teacher educators into their own identity and practice is indicative of the lack of certainty around the nature of the role. It also reflects the variability and transitional nature of professional identity in a field characterized by shifts and boundary crossing. This fluidity is articulated by teacher educator Mary Lynn Hamilton in her reflective discussion with Mieke Lunenberg: 'I think that my identity as a teacher educator is contextual. Sometimes I am a teacher, sometimes I am a teacher educator, sometimes I am a researcher, and sometimes I am professor. It depends on who I am with and what I want to accomplish' (Lunenberg and Hamilton, 2008: 186). Lunenberg, Korthagen and Zwart (2011) reference the concentration of self-study in North America and Australia and the relative paucity in European contexts outside of the UK, Scandinavian countries, Iceland and the Netherlands. In exploring the extent to which self-study research supported the development of teacher educators' professional identities, their analysis revealed four aspects of the development of a professional identity among the ten participating university-based teacher educators, identified as theoretical growth, greater awareness of an ongoing development, a shift towards the production of knowledge and growth in self-confidence (Lunenberg, Korthagen and Zwart, 2011: 412). Involvement in their project 'Teacher Educators Study Their Own Practices' helped the participating teacher educators to manage the transition from being a consumer of knowledge to a knowledge producer (Lunenberg and Hamilton, 2008), with the participants becoming increasingly active in contributing to the existing knowledge base on teacher education via the writing and dissemination of academic papers.

Identity is, therefore, a helpful lens for teacher educators as they attempt to reconcile the various aspects of their work. The necessity of managing conflicting roles and responsibilities in differing settings leads to the construction of 'repertoires of identities', with teacher educators embodying various identities according to the context and audience (Murray, Czerniawski and Barber, 2011: 270). Centring issues of identity gives a sense of cohesion, enabling the analysis of multiple roles and acknowledging the interplay between the personal and the professional. As Davey (2013) states, 'Identity is not a singularity but is better conceived as overlapping, dynamic, unstable and relative. It involves multiple 'selves', each continually re-constructed and re-expressed in the various personae and responsibilities taken on during the course of our work' (Davey, 2013: 117).

In their analysis of twenty-five journal articles published between 2000 and 2009 related to the identity and professional development of teacher educators, Swennen, Jones and Volman (2010) address the 'multiple selves' of teacher educators, identifying what they refer to as four 'sub-identities': teacher educators as school teachers, teacher educators as teachers in higher education, teacher educators as researchers and teacher educators as teachers of teachers. Drawing on the work of Holland et al. (1998), they note how these sub-identities are 'constructed within the various figured worlds teacher educators belong to simultaneously and at various moments in their careers' (Swennen, Jones and Volman, 2010: 143). These sub-identities are echoed in the findings of a study of university-based teacher educators in England conducted by Murray, Czerniawski and Barber (2011). Most of their participants associated strongly with an identity termed 'Once a school teacher', celebrating their past roles in schools as an integral part of their position in the university setting. The study also noted the tensions for teacher educators in embracing a researcher identity, with some teacher educators seeing themselves as 'aspirant researchers' and others distancing themselves from the role of knowledge construction, with research seen as 'not why we went into teacher training'. A later international survey by Czerniawski, Guberman and MacPhail (2017) found that the desire to gain research and academic writing skills was a common development need for teacher educators, as although teacher educators may be expected to be involved with research, they do not all feel confident and competent to conduct research (Smith and Flores, 2019).

Becoming a Teacher Educator – Managing Transition

> Becoming a teacher educator involves more than a job title. Developing an identity and practices in teacher education is best understood as a process of becoming. (Dinkelman, 2002: 4)

The development of an identity as a teacher educator is often associated with experiences of transition and change. Many transition to the role from previous work as school teachers, others hold different teaching positions in universities alongside their work supporting teachers. Some will experience the transition from one university setting to another, whereas others may move between schools or community locations. Griffiths, Thompson and Hryniewicz (2014) note that while the transfer from previous roles in schools is common in anglophone countries, in Israel and elsewhere, teacher educators are largely drawn from academic disciplines. Here the nature of transition involves the necessity of familiarization with the context of schools alongside the acquisition of pedagogical subject knowledge.

Moving from teacher to teacher educator is a common and potentially problematic transition (Murray and Male, 2005; Amott, 2018). In their review of self-studies conducted by teacher educators, Williams, Ritter and Bullock (2012: 250) conclude that 'a professional identity as a teacher educator is not the same as an identity as a classroom teacher, nor are they mutually exclusive.' This is evident in the self-study from Ritter (2007), whose transition from classroom teacher to teacher educator in a US university was partly characterized by a desire not to 'discredit' work as a teacher by selling out to higher education. Separation of the personal and professional often become blurred as teachers invest their 'selves' in their work (Nias, 1996). Any change in professional identity is therefore also a change in self and can result in what Warin et al. (2006: 237) term 'identity dissonance' – a 'psychological discomfort that can be felt when a person is aware of disharmonious experiences of self'.

Put simply, the variability of the role necessitates the management of transition in some form for all involved in teacher education. Such transitions can be a source of struggle, but also have the potential to alter 'one's sense of self' (Beach, 1999: 114). Past experiences inform future actions and relationships, captured in 'history-in-person', the 'sediment from past experiences upon which one improvises' (Holland et al., 1998: 18). These 'sediments' are inevitably rooted in different aspects of one's professional and personal history, impacting on the formation of professional identity: 'Identities constitute an enduring and significant aspect of history-in-person, history that is brought to current situations. They are the pivotal element of the perspective that persons bring to the construal of new activities and even new figured worlds' (Holland et al., 1998: 65).

Part of the challenge in transitioning to a teacher educator role comes in reconciling competing identities, a reflective and reflexive task that could be assisted further through engagement in focused induction and professional development activities.

The Identity and Role of Teacher Educators

Who is a teacher educator, what should they know and what do they do? (White, 2019: 200)

Answering this question is far from straightforward. Internationally, the range of people working in the field of teacher education is so varied that it is difficult to pinpoint the nature of the role across local, national and international contexts (Murray, Czerniawski and Kidd, n.d.). The problem of definition identified by Ducharme (1993) is exacerbated by the changing educational climate in which teacher educators are working. Subject to influences from personal, social, cultural and institutional contexts, the role is also impacted by political policy, creating instability and uncertainty.

A generic definition is provided by the European Commission (2013), drawing on the work of a Thematic Working Group 'Teacher Professional Development' comprising experts nominated by twenty-six European countries and stakeholder organizations: 'Teacher Educators are all those who actively facilitate the (formal) learning of student teachers and teachers' (European Commission, 2013: 8).

While this definition is sufficiently broad to encompass a variety of contexts where teacher education is enacted, its focus is on the facilitation of learning rather than acknowledging the importance of teaching about teaching – the pedagogy of teacher education (Korthagen, 2016; Loughran, 2006). The articulation of the complex nature of teaching (Loughran and Menter, 2019) requires professional knowledge that moves beyond facilitation.

A more nuanced overview is provided by Goodwin et al. (2014: 285) who describe the teacher educator as someone with a 'purposeful commitment to a professional life that is centered on the teaching of teachers and a deep understanding of what it means to teach about teaching'. This definition addresses the pedagogical aspects of the role, but the word 'centered' is problematic. Many teacher educators have other roles too, working in schools or in communities. Some may not even identify themselves as teacher educators. As noted by the European Commission (2013),

Research suggests that teacher educators, unlike members of other professions, have multiple professional identities: they may think of themselves primarily as school teachers, as teachers in higher education, as researchers, or as teachers of teachers (Swennen, Jones and Volman, 2010) – or they may identify with several of these roles simultaneously. Many of those who teach teachers might not consider themselves to be teacher educators at all. (European Commission, 2013: 8)

These multiple roles are inevitably embedded in cultural and political national contexts, further complicating considerations of identity in the professional lives of teacher educators. As Rodgers and Scott (2008: 733) assert, 'Identity is dependent upon and formed within multiple contexts which bring social, cultural, political, and historical forces to bear upon that formation.'

Teacher Educator Identity in Context

The environment where teacher educators work inevitably impacts on the formation of professional identity. Subgroups defined by location can be identified, each with its own 'identity, role, career trajectory and professional learning needs', each of which brings 'issues of self-identification and recognition' (White, 2019: 202).

University-Based Teacher Educators

Despite the huge amount of self-study research authored by university-based teacher educators, Ellis and McNicholl (2015) highlight the lack of attention in the literature to the precise nature of teacher educators' work in universities. Their analysis of job advertisements and job descriptions for teacher education vacancies in England during 2008–9 revealed a focus on the noun 'practitioner' and the inclusion of desirable personal qualities pertaining to enthusiasm and dedication. Although teaching was emphasized, many advertisements referenced training and delivering content. Notably, references to research as part of the role were absent for 45 per cent of the advertisements. Instead, a teaching identity dominated: 'The HEIs commonly conceptualized the teacher educator as a *super teacher*, a skilled classroom practitioner but a practitioner who possesses considerable personal qualities, such as enthusiasm and resilience' (Ellis and McNicholl, 2015: 56–7).

In a replication of the study in Australia, Nuttall et al. (2013: 337) found similar references to personal qualities pertaining to enthusiasm and excellence, but also noted a surprising absence of specific references to the term teacher educator, 'although terms such as "teaching" and "educator" peppered these texts, "teacher educator" as a category of academic work was almost never named.' Such textual avoidance further highlights the challenges in identifying and developing the professional identities of teacher educators and the tensions that exist in centring their role in universities.

It is not uncommon for university-based teacher educators to begin their career in schools, and many studies have highlighted the difficulties that the transition from school teacher to university-based teacher educator can present (Murray, 2005; Zeichner, 2005). This movement has been conceptualized as a change from *first-order practitioners*, working as schoolteachers in the first-order setting of the school, to *second-order practitioners*, working as teacher educators in the second-order setting of the university (Murray and Male, 2005). Such a transition can also result in a change in status as teachers who were in senior positions in schools can find themselves recast from expert to novice in the higher education environment. Conversely, Amott's (2018) study conducted with six neophyte teacher educators transitioning to their university-based role from careers teaching in schools revealed a strong affinity with an 'expert' identity: 'Whilst the identity as a teacher educator was less well developed, a sense of expertise, as a teacher, subject specialist or Reading Recovery teacher, was supportive for them in their new role and provided sufficient strength of identity to enable them to transition more effectively' (Amott, 2018: 483).

Although the participants did not identify a 'teacher educator' identity in their narratives, some of the indicators of 'identity as an expert' (including evidence of skills and knowledge, self-belief and future aspirations) were similar to those of teacher educator identity and separate from previous 'teacher' identities. That said, it is important to recognize the differing nature of the roles. As Zeichner (2005) reminds us, 'one's expertise as a teacher does not necessarily translate into expertise as a mentor of teachers' (Zeichner, 2005: 118), echoing Feiman-Nemser's (2001) claim that good teachers are not necessarily good teacher educators.

School-Based Teacher Educators

Internationally, a turn towards practice in teacher education (Zeichner and Bier, 2015) has seen the increased involvement of schools in the development of teachers. This is particularly apparent in pre-service teacher education. In England, the emergence of many different routes into teaching has fundamentally altered the pre-service teacher education landscape, resulting in significant changes to the positioning of universities in the preparation of teachers. With responsibility for the training of teachers increasingly moving away from higher education and towards schools, the contributors to the discourses of teacher preparation are changing. White (2019) cites the prioritization of teachers over teacher educators in policy documents in Australia, noting how reforms to pre-service teacher education processes have placed a greater degree of responsibility on teachers in schools for the preparation of teachers, necessitating the simultaneous embodiment of a 'dual role' as teacher and teacher educator. McIntyre, Youens and Stevenson (2017: 2) claim that in England, 'Since 2010, university voices have been systematically marginalized and, in some cases, silenced in debates about teacher preparation and policies have actively reduced their input.'

Despite the increased focus on the role of teacher educators in schools, the representation of this group in the literature is underdeveloped in comparison with those working in the university setting. Teacher educators in schools are not always recognized as being anything other than teachers and may not consider themselves to be teacher educators either (Swennen, Jones and Volman, 2010; Livingston, 2014). In many countries, collaboration between higher education institutions and other training providers and mentor teachers in schools is pivotal to the development of teachers, and yet research into the identity development of mentor teachers in schools is sparse (Izadinia, 2014; Murray and Male, 2005). The adoption of the dual role of teacher and teacher educator has been shown to result in multiple professional loyalties among mentor teachers (Feiman-Nemser, 2001), some of which may be conflicting. Identification as a teacher educator can be completely absent, as evident in Livingston and Shiach's (2013) study involving fifty mentors working in primary and secondary schools in Scotland: 'The analysis of the mentors' reflections on their role showed that they took up roles as a: teacher; resource; facilitator; observer; collaborator; listener; enquiry partner; and problem-solver. The term "teacher educator" was not used in the list of roles they identified' (Livingston, 2014: 225).

Through their investigation into the professional identity of mentor teachers partnered with two universities in Norway, Andreasen, Bjørndal and Kovač (2019) offer a theoretical framework to specify the processes that are important for the development of a teacher educator identity among mentor teachers. Their findings highlight the necessity of collaborative cultures within schools and how collaboration between schools and university partners aids the development of a teacher educator identity among mentor teachers. Such practices can also impact positively on well-being and feelings of inclusion. Collaborative practice will be discussed further in Chapter 5, but it is important to note the inherent challenges in the fragmentary and complex nature of the mentor role.

Community-Based Teacher Educators

Community-based educators are defined by White (2019) as comprising those drawn from the larger school community and encompasses parents and key community groups. She cites examples from a range of Canadian based studies, noting the indigenous nature of such educators in both Canada and Australia. Navigating the 'third' or 'hybrid' space (Williams, 2013; Zeichner, 2015) between universities, schools and communities serves to illuminate the diversity of teacher educator identities. Drawing on the conceptualization of 'third space' by Gutierrez, Norton-Meier and Drake (2010) sought to understand the interactions of pre-service teachers in the overlapping spaces provided by homes, universities, schools and communities. Their findings point to an understanding of space that transcends the physicality of the library and seeks to address issues around the formation of a professional identity. This view is supported by Zeichner, Payne and Brayko (2015) who describe a 'critical time' for teacher education, with a need for the utilization of 'hybrid' spaces, where schools, universities and communities can work together to support teacher learning outside of traditional hierarchies. Generally, this aspect of teacher education remains underdeveloped in the literature, and as noted by Guillen and Zeichner (2018), there is a need for further research into community-based teacher education programmes, focusing on how community partnerships can be built and sustained.

Teacher Educators in Post-Compulsory Education

If you are teaching in further education, community development learning, workplace learning, 14–19 provision, public services training or offender learning which is not delivered by school teachers, you are working in post-compulsory education. (Crawley, 2010: 14)

Labelled as 'the invisible educators' (Thurston, 2010), teacher educators in this sector have been characterized as the 'outsiders' of the teacher education world' (Crawley, 2013: 346), and it is a group that is severely under-represented in the literature (Springbett, 2018). It is not uncommon for those working in this sector to have been recruited based on prior experience in industry or commerce rather than for teaching expertise, and the job often encompasses managerial positions alongside teaching (Springbett, 2018). As Crawley (2013) states, there is a diversity and breadth in post-compulsory education (PCE) that separates the sector from other contexts: 'Respondents mentioned the bewildering range of situations, contexts, theories, approaches, methodologies, policies and dimensions of practice they work with in the PCE and the equally diverse range of trainees they support' (Crawley, 2013: 344).

This diversity inevitably impacts on the formation of a teacher educator identity, and in the situated context of local contentious practice (Holland and Lave, 2001), tensions are apparent. In her socioculturally framed study of PCE-based teacher educators in England, Springbett (2018) found that the political context of the environment significantly influenced the teacher educators' work and identities, with frequent restructuring increasing workload and reframing practice. There was a liminal sense to the participants' teacher educator identity, considering themselves 'both teachers and different from other teachers' (Springbett, 2018: 157) and 'inhabiting a no-man's land between the cultures of their colleges and university partners' (Springbett, 2018: 156). These findings highlight the relevance of context when examining identity, with Springbett noting the limiting nature of market forces and institutional performance targets on the development of a teacher identity in the PCE sector.

Teacher Educators in 'New Graduate Schools of Education'

In their presentation of teacher educators as entrepreneurial reformers, Cochran-Smith, Keefe and Carney (2018) describe a 'new cadre' of teacher educators located in what they term, 'new graduate schools of education' (nGSEs), defined as, 'new independent organizations that offer teacher preparation programs and use university language, such as "graduate school of education" (GSE) and "dean," but are not affiliated with universities' (Cochran-Smith, Keefe and Carney, 2018: 575).

Characterized by a desire to disrupt existing practices of teacher preparation (namely those housed within US universities), teacher educators in this context promote a prescriptive practice-based approach, modelled on specific pedagogical moves and dismissive of more theoretical approaches. Cochran-Smith, Keefe and Carney (2018) note examples of similar practice in private teacher education providers in Ireland, Israel and England, as demonstrated in Ellis, Steadman and Trippestad's (2019) analysis of the Institute for Teaching, an organization in England that was modelled on the Independent Graduate Schools of Education in the United States and built on the pedagogical premise that the role of the teacher educator is to provide opportunities for teachers to master an identified set of core instructional techniques.

Though not exhaustive, the above categorization of teacher educators by location highlight the situated nature of professional identity and the influence by the values and discourse of a given setting. Professional identity becomes associated with specific ways of thinking and acting in various participative and collaborative worlds. For example, the figured world of teacher education in the nGSE is framed by a view of traditional university teacher preparation as a 'problem' that can be solved by relocating to a practically orientated environment (Cochran-Smith, Keefe and Carney, 2018).

Professional Development

The varied professional backgrounds of teacher educators highlight the lack of a formal route into the profession. As Goodwin and Kosnik (2013: 338–9) observe, 'With little in the way of preparation, new teacher educators are left to invent their practice, to learn on the job, often in isolation.' Izadinia's (2014) analysis of fifty-two research studies found challenges for teacher educators in developing a professional identity, with negative self-views arising from a lack of confidence in knowledge and abilities to perform the role, exacerbated by the lack of high-quality induction and support programmes. Her review revealed a consensus around the need for four key features in induction programmes, each focused on the development of professional identity: induction programmes to act as learning communities for new teacher educators, these communities to establish supportive collegial relationships between participants, the provision of reflective activities enabling identity construction and opportunities for practitioner research and self-enquiry. As has been discussed, there are additional challenges for teacher educators working in schools, PCE and other settings. As Berry (2016) observes, 'There seems a strange discrepancy between, on the one hand, a pressing need to prepare high-quality teachers, and on the other, a relative lack of organised preparation for those whose responsibility it is to prepare these future teachers' (Berry, 2016: 40).

The absence of supportive, coherent induction practices (Murray, Czerniawski and Barber, 2011; Kosnik et al., 2015a) results in many teacher educators learning 'on the job' (Grossman, 1990) and 'on their own' (Berry, 2016: 39). Research conducted by Mitchell and Joseph (2021) with teacher educators in Trinidad and Tobago revealed how emotive responses to a lack of focused training and support can become, as evident in the words of one of their university-based teacher educator participants:

> I do not think there is any recognition of the need to prepare teacher educators in our system. I do not think there is anything in place to foster and maintain their skills. I do not think there is any real understanding or recognition of what a teacher educator is. There is no programme of development for preparing subject specialists who are hired. (Mitchell and Joseph, 2021: 193)

Despite the documented fragmentary nature of professional development provision for teacher educators, there is evidence of successful practice. Smith and Flores (2019) highlight a number of European, national and local initiatives addressing the professional development of teacher educators, including the European collaborative International Forum for Teacher Educator Development (InFo-TED), The MOFET Institute in Israel, the Dutch Association for Teacher Educators (VELON) in the Netherlands and the Norwegian National Research School in Teacher Education (NAFOL) in Norway.

InFo-TED

InFo-TED is an international forum of teacher educators working to support the professional development of all teacher educators. Current members are from England, Flanders/Belgium, Ireland, Israel, Netherlands, Norway, Scotland, Australia and the United States. The forum's stance on the development of teacher educators is practice based, stemming from the belief that 'teacher educators' sense of professional self or identity needs to be seen as reflected in their actions' (Kelchtermans, Smith and Vanderlinde, 2018: 125). This is captured in the InFo-TED conceptual

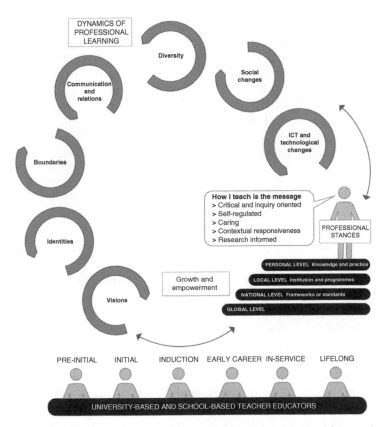

FIGURE 1 *Conceptual model for teacher educators' professional development.*

Note: Reproduced with kind permission of Critical Publishing from Teacher Educators in the Twenty-First Century (2018) by Gerry Czerniawski.

model on teacher educators' professional development, depicted in Figure 1.

The model is designed to offer a shared language for research, discussion and the development of practice across institutional and international borders. The model acknowledges the differing contexts of teacher educators' work and the fact that teacher educators enter the teacher education profession from different places and at different moments in their careers. As such, there is much variability in both experience and learning needs. In addressing identity, it forefronts a view of teacher educators as professionals, with the concentric circles reflecting the movement and dynamics of professional learning, as well as its inevitable 'situated-ness' in contexts specific to the individual (Kelchtermans, Smith and Vanderlinde, 2018: 127).

MOFET Institute in Israel

Founded in 1983 by the Department of Teacher Education of the Israeli Ministry of Education, the MOFET Institute in Israel is a national intercollegiate centre for the research and development of curricula and programmes in teacher education and teaching in the colleges. MOFET's stated mission is to 'serve as a professional meeting-place and to facilitate an educational dialogue among colleagues both in the teacher education system and in other settings in the education system' (https://mofet-web.macam.ac.il/international/mofet-institute/). Its online academy provides a framework for the acquisition of knowledge and the sharing of professional practice across a wide range of people involved in teacher education, including teacher educators and teachers, researchers of education and teaching, educational policymakers and educational leaders. The promotion of such communities of practice combines with the provision of webinars, seminars, professional visits and conferences.

VELON in the Netherlands

In the Netherlands, the VELON has devised a 'Knowledge Base for Teacher Educators' built around seven focus areas, listed on their website (https://velon.nl/) as

1. The teacher educator
2. The context of teacher education
3. Subject content and teaching methodology
4. Educating together in the school
5. Research in teacher education programmes
6. Training in teacher education
7. Training didactics: how do we educate teachers?

Voluntary professional registration is linked to satisfaction of a Professional Standard for Teacher Educators, designed as an instrument for making the quality of the Dutch teacher education profession more transparent (Koster and Dengerink, 2008).

NAFOL in Norway

NAFOL is a national research school offering specialized education and training in preschool, school and teacher education. Coordinated by the Faculty of Social Sciences and Technology Management, at the Norwegian University of Science and Technology, NAFOL is organized as a partnership between seven Norwegian universities and twelve university colleges. Established in 2010, the school aims to promote research by teacher educators by developing a research-based knowledge base for teacher education, strengthening institutional research activities, including training for teacher educators in the supervising of student teachers' research projects (Smith and Flores, 2019).

Other initiatives include online courses such as the 'Becoming a Teacher Educator' course offered by the Teacher Education Advancement Network in the UK. Aimed at those in the first three years of a teacher educator role, the course comprises modules on aspects of teacher education pedagogy, partnership, advanced scholarship, and research. In Australia, guidance is offered by the Australian Institute for Teaching and School Leadership for those teachers supporting the induction of newcomers to the profession, including the provision of an app entitled 'My Induction' for use with beginning teachers in schools. There are many other examples of such practices internationally, but overall, the literature highlights a lack of coherence and visibility around teacher educators' professional learning, despite broad agreement that professional learning aids the development of the teacher educator identity.

Conclusion

Teacher education is of its very nature Janus-faced. In one direction it faces classroom and school, with the demands for relevance, practicality, competence, techniques. In the other it faces university and the world of research, with their stress on scholarship, theoretical fruitfulness and disciplinary rigour. (Taylor, 1983: 41)

The conceptualization of teacher education as Janus-faced captures the often conflicting and always complex nature of teacher educator professional identity. Teacher educators can be caught in a two-worlds paradox (Olsen and Buchanan, 2017), working at the intersection of the contrasting worlds of the university and the world of schools. Much of the literature points to the need for cohesive induction and professional development provision for teacher educators to ease such tensions. In their White Paper titled 'The Importance of Teacher Educators: Professional Development Imperatives', InFo-TED (2019: 8) bemoan the lack of sufficient acknowledgement for teacher educators by policymakers, concluding, 'There is then a need for national, European and wider international cooperation to disseminate the awareness that "Teacher Educators Matter".' Focused professional learning can positively influence professional identity development, but it is apparent that the diverse nature of teacher educators requires a diverse approach to both induction and professional development that is contextually situated and responsive to individual needs.

CHAPTER FOUR

Identity in Practice

Teacher educator professional identities are uncertain and complex, but engaging with issues of identity is a way of participating in and thinking about practice, connecting what teacher educators think and do. This chapter addresses how the development of teacher educators' practice is inextricably linked to the development of their professional identity, despite a lack of certainty around what teacher educators should know and be able to do. In considering identity in practice, the necessity of learning from the intersectional nature of identity is addressed.

Key Points

- The transitionary nature of practice for many teacher educators and the presence of 'multiple selves' (Davey, 2013);

- difficulties in pinpointing a knowledge base for teacher educators and the relevance of the development of a pedagogy of teacher education (Loughran and Menter, 2019; Shulman, 2005);

- the limited demographic diversity in teacher education and the need for teacher educators' work to promote

educational equity and social justice through
intersectionality-minded practice.

Identity and Practice

Engaging with issues of identity is a way of participating in and
thinking about practice. In reviewing the literature on teacher
educator identity, Izadinia (2014) states that 'the development of
a professional identity has been recognised as a central process in
becoming a teacher educator because there is a close connection
between identity and practice. In other words, the development
of teacher educators' practice is connected to the development
of their professional identity' (Izadinia, 2014: 427).

There is a necessarily political dimension to the identity
construction of those working in education, with practice
framed by the enduring struggles of the localized context
(Holland and Lave, 2001). Olsen and Buchanan (2017)
discuss the tension for teacher educators in working at the
'intersection' of the often conflicting worlds of the university
and the school environment. Their US-based research revealed
the complexity for teacher educators in trying to reconcile
competing epistemologies: 'Practice, according to these teacher
educators, is a kind of tug-of-war between the constructivist
learning approaches espoused in the university and the
scripted-curricula, testing, behaviorist, and didactic-instruction
pressures dominating many of the participating K–12 schools'
(Olsen and Buchanan, 2017: 26).

Many nations have experienced a turn towards practice
(Zeichner and Bier, 2015) in teacher education, with national
education policies increasingly emphasizing practical teaching
strategies. In England, political discourses around teacher
education place little value on the role of universities. Instead,
an 'on the job' (Grossman, 1990; Cochran-Smith, 2005)
approach to the development of teachers prioritizes school-
led systems over the traditional home of teacher education in

higher education institutions. This changing epistemology of teacher education has left some educators struggling with a cultural change in which their professional agency is reduced and their emotional response is likely to include frustration. A more agentic stance is presented by Cochran-Smith, Keefe and Carney (2018). Noting how reforms of initial teacher education programmes, policies and practices in the United States have positioned teachers and teacher educators as the objects of reform, they re-conceptualize teacher educators as the *agents* of reform, analysing approaches that are 'initiated, developed, and promoted by teacher educators themselves' (Cochran-Smith, Keefe and Carney, 2018: 572).

As discussed in Chapter 3, it is not uncommon for teacher educators in higher education settings to have had previous professional experience in schools. Occupational change from school teaching to teacher education can result in identity shifts and professional uncertainty (Czerniawski, 2018), as practice is re-framed. Inevitably, understanding of the role of teaching has been developed through practical experience of the classroom and interaction with students and colleagues in the school setting. The relevance of this experiential knowledge to the teacher educator role is clear, but it is also individualized. Rooted in the realities of school life, the teacher professional identity is also replete with personal beliefs about the nature of teaching, informed in part by having experienced the process of becoming a teacher.

In their study of twenty-eight teacher educators in England, Murray and Male (2005: 129) encountered high levels of stress and anxiety among their interviewees undergoing such transitions, noting that the path to becoming a teacher educator was a 'slow, uncertain process'. For the majority of the teacher educators involved in their study, it took between two and three years to establish a new professional identity as a teacher educator, despite having established careers in schools. This transition is presented in terms of the situational and substantial self (Nias, 1989):

Situational selves are developed from interaction with others whilst the substantial self is a core of self-defining beliefs relatively impervious to change, many of which are formed through general life experiences. This does not deny the potential for the substantial self to be affected by changes in life experiences, however, and being reframed in accord with altered circumstances. (Murray and Male, 2005: 126–7)

The career transition is seen as complete when the situational and substantial selves are closely aligned, resulting in a confidence in the new position.

Many researchers have cited the need for improved induction for teacher educators (Murray, Czerniawski and Barber, 2011; Kosnik et al., 2015a), providing structured preparation as opposed to seeing teacher education as a 'self-evident activity' (Zeichner, 2005: 118). Enabling conscious and considered reflection at times of transition could help alleviate some of the stresses of change, inviting analysis of personally held beliefs and assumptions. As Murray and Male (2005: 139) highlight, this approach can serve to validate the pedagogical expertise enacted in the school context, acknowledging how previous practices inform professional identity and helping to align the situational and substantial selves.

Multiple Identities in Practice

The conceptualization of the teacher educator identity in their practice is considered by Davey (2013). His research conducted with teacher educators in New Zealand comprised the conducting and analysing of interviews to reveal metaphorical clusters that link to the conceptualization of the teacher educator identity and their practice. These are identified as

- Metaphors of life and living – teacher educator as lived life;
- Metaphors of journey and exploration – teacher educator as fellow traveller;

- Metaphors of construction, design and building – teacher educator as architect;
- Metaphors of ecology, generativeness, and growth – teacher educator as gardener-environmentalist;
- Metaphors of nurturing, nutrition, and relationships – teacher educator as carer.

(Davey, 2013: 119)

Teacher educator as 'lived life' emphasizes the centrality of teaching in the activity of teacher educators. Linked with feelings of personal fulfilment and value, this identity construction highlights the emotionality of teaching and the close personal identification with teaching as a profession (Nias, 1996). Murray, Czerniawski and Barber (2011) note how for teacher educators moving from schools into university settings, the identity of 'once a school teacher' remains very present, even after several years away from the school classroom. Teacher educator as 'fellow traveller' speaks to notions of transition and journey, a sense of 'becoming' and growth in pedagogy, theoretical understanding and professional relationships. Teacher educator as 'architect' emphasizes the building of a career on the foundations of teaching and the way in which teacher educators come to construct experiences for those they work with, filling in gaps and shaping responses. The conceptualization of teacher educator as 'gardener-environmentalist' arose from predictable images in Davey's data of growth and nurturing but also alludes to the broader interactive nature of the teacher education experience. Communities of practice link fellow teacher educators across spaces, forming networks with teachers and pupils in schools. Finally, the view of teacher educators as 'carer' centres the ethical, moral and value-laden nature of the work. Responsibility is presented both as a nurturing necessity and a desire to encourage independence through challenge and questioning. Davey also highlights the presence of tensions in reconciling the often competing aspects of the professional role, including the emotional tension presented by a need to both support and challenge students.

Knowledge, Pedagogy and Identity

While it is widely acknowledged that the practice of teacher education is linked with the development of the professional identity, there remains a lack of certainty about exactly what teacher educators should know and do. As with teaching, the knowledge base is neither fixed nor finite, and although it has been described as commonsensical that quality teacher education is reliant on quality teacher educators (Goodwin et al., 2014), the nature of what teacher educators should know and do is poorly articulated. Combine this with a paucity of structured induction into the role and it becomes inevitable that teacher educators will draw on their own experiences, engaging with their substantial self and potentially reproducing rather than challenging their own institutional biography (Britzman, 2003). As Goodwin et al. (2014: 296) comment, 'Without a discrete and identifiable knowledge-(base)-for-practice, those who teach teachers can only teach as they were taught.'

In their study of 293 university-based teacher educators in the United States, Goodwin et al. (2014) draw on the three conceptions of teacher learning and knowing advanced by Cochran-Smith and Lytle (1999) in their theorizing of the relationships of knowledge and practice. The lenses of knowledge-for-practice, knowledge-in-practice and knowledge-of-practice are adopted as useful heuristics for describing essential knowledge for teacher educators. Acknowledging that there are essential differences between teachers and teacher educators, they see commonalities between skills and competencies for teaching and for teacher educating in providing insight into the practice of teacher education. Cochran-Smith and Lytle's three conceptions are outlined below.

Knowledge-for-Practice

Knowledge-for-practice refers to the formal knowledge and theory necessary for teachers to use to improve practice. This body of knowledge includes subject knowledge, assessment, learning theories and knowledge of the teaching profession. This conception 'hinges on the idea that knowing more ... leads more or less directly to more effective practice' (Cochran-Smith and Lytle, 1999: 254). One of the most influential approaches to examining a knowledge base for teacher educators is the work of Lee Shulman. Categorizing a knowledge base for teachers, Shulman identifies seven categories of teacher knowledge, including knowledge of subject matter, pedagogy and curriculum; knowledge of learners and their characteristics; and knowledge of educational contexts. Pedagogical content knowledge (PCK), defined as 'that special amalgam of content and pedagogy that is uniquely the province of teachers, their own special form of professional understanding' (Shulman, 1987: 8), is singled out by Shulman as being of particular interest. As noted by Berry, Depaepe and van Driel (2016), Shulman's conceptualization of PCK has been criticized for presenting a static view of teacher knowledge. However, such criticism negates the centrality of context, as highlighted by Shulman himself: 'PCK was not to be construed as "something" that teachers had in their heads but was a more dynamic construct that described the processes that teachers employed when confronted with the challenge of teaching particular subjects to particular learners in specific settings' (Shulman, 2015: 9).

In these terms, PCK can be seen as the 'professional knowledge that each teacher develops on the basis of his/her experiences during teacher education and in practice' (Berry, Depaepe and van Driel, 2016: 349), a conceptualization linked to both context and professional identity.

Although usually associated with the distinctive knowledge for teaching associated with classroom practice, PCK is as pertinent to teacher educators. There are many empirical studies on PCK in pre-service teacher education from around the world, particularly relating to science and mathematics (e.g. Turnuklu and Yesildere, 2007; Loughran, Mulhall and Berry, 2008). In her conceptualization of Shulman's model, Grossman (1990) centres on four elements of PCK – conceptions of purposes for teaching subject matter, knowledge of students' understanding, curricular knowledge and knowledge of instructional strategies – concluding that 'teacher education courses can provide a context for the re-examination of subject matter from a purposefully pedagogical perspective and help prospective teachers develop conceptions of what it means to teach their subject matter to diverse students' (Grossman, 1990: 143).

Knowledge-in-Practice

In contrast, knowledge-in-practice is situated in the practical experience of teaching. It assumes that novice teachers learn when they are given opportunities to observe and reflect on the work of expert teachers and through deliberative reflection on their own interactions in the classroom. Through such reflections, learning is integrated, internalized and personalized. Rather than existing outside of schools, knowledge-in-practice is situated within the teaching profession, positioning teachers as the designers and architects of action and thus the generators of knowledge. This emphasis on the practical is equally pertinent to teacher education, where practice is formed both in formal sites of learning, such as universities, and in the varied communities where teacher educators work. As Kosnik et al. (2015b: 218) observe, 'As a community of teacher educators, we need to be learning from each other about successful pedagogical practices.'

Knowledge-of-Practice

Thirdly, knowledge-of-practice bridges the gap between knowledge-for-practice and knowledge-in-practice. This career-long 'pedagogic act' sees classrooms as the sites for intentional investigation, with teachers linking practical knowledge to wider theory, making their classrooms and schools 'sites for inquiry' (Cochran-Smith and Lytle, 1999: 273). This is not a synthesis of the preceding two, but instead transcends the formal-practical dichotomy to position knowledge as collectively constructed through inquiry as teachers problematize their own knowledge and that of others. Again, this inquiry stance is as relevant to teacher educators as classroom teachers, encapsulated in the concept of a pedagogy of teacher education.

A Pedagogy of Teacher Education

An ability to articulate the professional knowledge of teaching about teaching is addressed through the development of a pedagogy of teacher education (Loughran, 2006, 2011; Korthagen, 2016; Loughran and Menter, 2019). There is a fundamental difference between teaching and teaching about teaching, with the latter calling on a knowledge base and skill set that requires teacher educators to be more than good classroom teachers. As Loughran (2006: 19) comments, 'A pedagogy of teacher education ... inevitably impacts on a teacher educator's identity.'

Reflecting the movement from the position of a *first-order practitioner* to a *second-order practitioner* (Murray and Male, 2005), or from teaching to teaching about teaching (Loughran, 2006), such pedagogical transitions require a reformulation of professional identity. The development of a scholarship of teacher education through engagement with high-quality research into and about teacher education (Menter, 2018) informs the practice of teacher educators, demonstrating pedagogical expertise and enacting the capacity to influence the future direction of the field. As Loughran and Menter (2019: 226) state, 'Teacher educators need to be seen as scholars with the knowledge, skills and ability to shape policy and practice in ways that will move us beyond the status quo.' They argue that the role of teacher educators in constructing and shaping a knowledge base results in a movement away from preparation for classroom readiness to the professional development of pedagogical expertise. Development of such a pedagogy of teacher education can be helpfully informed by research conducted within the profession.

Pedagogical ideas are developed further in Shulman's later work. In 'Signature Pedagogies in the Professions', he defines signature pedagogies as 'the forms of instruction that leap to mind when we first think about the preparation of members of particular professions.' (Shulman, 2005: 52). Shulman draws examples from medicine and the law to highlight the intuitive nature of such signature pedagogies. For example, he cites the 'bedside teaching' approach during the clinical rounds of a senior physician instructing student medics. Speaking against the varied practice in teacher education, demonstrative of a field that 'can't get its act together', Shulman advocates the adoption of signature pedagogies as 'systematic ways of preparing professionals' (in Falk, 2006: 76). In the field of teacher education, such recurrent routines may include inquiry, focused observation, mentoring, co-teaching, reflection and integrating coursework with fieldwork (Yendol-Hoppey and Franco, 2014: 21). While Shulman (2005: 56) acknowledges that signature pedagogies will 'necessarily distort learning in some manner', he also emphasizes that they are pedagogies of uncertainty and that learning to deal with the uncertainty of students in classrooms is a fundamental aspect of professionalism. There is also recognition of the emotionality of learning, with the emotive experience of teaching and learning influencing the 'values, dispositions, and characters of those who learn' (Shulman, 2005: 57–8).

Reflecting on the relevance of Shulman's model, Knight (2021) identifies a number of signature pedagogies for teacher education, including collaboration with experienced teachers and peers, inquiry into one's own practice and observation of and dialogue with experienced teachers. In suggesting a focus on complex core practices such as modelling, he also emphasizes that this should not be seen as 'isolating a series of micro-routines to build a fixed repertoire which fit one specific school or class'. It is this focus on the generic that appears to characterize modern policy in teacher education, resulting in a 'narrow and mechanistic' view of effective teaching (Falk, 2006: 78).

The Impact on Identity

These varied knowledge and pedagogical approaches have a direct impact on the development of teacher educators' identity. The content and method of delivery on teacher education courses inevitably influences perspectives on teaching and teachers, and teacher educators can find themselves ensnared by a simplified view in policy of what it means to teach that conflicts with their own multiplicity of identities and beliefs. Internationally, a move towards a 'technical-rational' approach to teaching (Schön, 1987) has promoted concepts of 'classroom-ready teachers' (TEMAG, 2014) and an observed shift in teacher education from 'preparing "highly qualified teachers" to preparing "highly effective teachers"' (Cochran-Smith et al., 2011: 19). This 'how-to' approach to practice is synonymous with a practical approach to education. As Deborah Lowenberg Ball comments, 'We study and improve education practice. By education practice, we mean the doing of education' (Jesse, 2016). Ball joins Grossman, Hammerness and McDonald (2009) in advocating that teacher education be structured around a set of 'core practices' for teaching that are taught to novice teachers. The core practice movement arises from a conviction that teacher education, 'requires a shift from a focus on what teachers know and believe to a greater focus on what teachers do' (Ball and Forzani, 2009: 503).

Critics of the core practices approach argue that a focus on generic methods fails to address the needs of the individual, with teacher preparation becoming conceptualized as teacher *training* rather than the *education* of teachers. Issues of equity and social justice are foregrounded as the call for 'deliberate and unabashed prescriptiveness' (Ball and Forzani, 2009: 506) is perceived as separating the teachers' practice from their own cultural and social identities: 'This separation strips individual teachers of both their resources for connecting with children through shared culture and identities and their accountability for bridging the differences between themselves and the students they teach' (Philip et al., 2018: 257).

A training model has affinity with the view of teacher identity as craftworker or technician (Zeichner, 2012; Orchard and Winch, 2015). There is a neatness in its focus on skills acquisition. As Crawford (2017: 199) comments, 'The training route is very seductive; it offers a common-sense argument that points to what populist rhetoric assumes are the skills that teachers need.' However, a training model does little to address the emotional and social nature of teaching. In contrast, teacher education, and in particular the development of pedagogical expertise by teacher educators, suggests the development of theory-embedded practice and the ongoing process of learning both about teaching and self-identity.

We have seen how the professional identity of teacher educators is a fluid conception, incorporating personal biography and experience as well as developing in response to specific contexts and relationships. There is a danger that such variation and individuality is stifled by the imposition of specified ways of working, evidenced in an increasingly controlling policy agenda in the international field of teacher education. Goodwin and Kosnik (2013) reference the ongoing debates around the nature of teacher education in the United States, citing the tensions between models favouring the practical acquisition of skills through clinical practice (such as Lemov, 2010) and a contrasting view of learning to teach as complex and dynamic, requiring specialized knowledge. In England, the increasingly centralized control of initial teacher education is exemplified by the introduction of the Core Content Framework (DfE, 2019a) for pre-service teachers and Early Career Framework (DfE, 2019b) for teachers in their first two years in the profession, prescribing the knowledge and skills that teachers should have. An emphasis on cognitive science and the power of memory permeates both frameworks, along with an assumption that all pre-service teachers will learn in the same way and at the same pace. Pedagogy is prescribed though a series of 'learn how to' statements that detail the minimum entitlements of those learning to teach. The subsequent market review of initial teacher training (GOV.UK, 2021) includes the advocation of a 'rigorous sequencing of the training curriculum so that trainees' knowledge and expertise are built systematically across the course'. Such prescription can be seen to de-professionalize teacher educators, synonymous with their characterization as technicians rather than critical, reflective professionals (Zeichner, 2012; Orchard and Winch, 2015). Missing in the policy documentation is the exploration of teacher identity and what it means to be a teacher, framed around such questions as 'Who am I as a teacher?' and 'What kind of teacher do I want to become?' (Beijaard and Meijer, 2017: 177). The prescription of pedagogical practice sits in opposition to the fluid conceptions of identity and an embracing of the multiple selves at work in the practice of teacher education.

Intersectionality-Minded Practice

Identity is intersectional. The recognition of the interconnected nature of multiple identities formed and enacted in distinctive social, historical and cultural locations informs understandings of privilege and power and their impact on practice. The term 'intersectionality' was coined by Kimberlé Crenshaw (1989), and in an interview conducted two decades later, she reflects on its meaning:

> Intersectionality is a lens through which you can see where power comes and collides, where it interlocks and intersects. It's not simply that there's a race problem here, a gender problem here, and a class or LBGTQ problem there. Many times that framework erases what happens to people who are subject to all of these things. (Columbia Law School, 2017)

Pugach, Gomez-Najarro and Matewos's (2019: 213) review of empirical research on social justice in teacher education reveals that identity is often presented in a unidimensional manner, with the 'relative invisibility of intersectionality' perhaps speaking to a lack of familiarity among teacher educators. Bešić (2020: 116) presents the multifaceted nature of intersectionality in the metaphor of an 'intersection onion'. At the core is the individual, possessing multiple overlapping identities simultaneously, impacting both on how they see themselves and how they view and interact with society. The next layer pertains to group memberships, showing how 'individuals perceived to be the same are categorized together as members of one particular group'. Membership of a group is neither exclusive nor fixed. Moving outwards in the onion layer, 'Social Context' addresses society's categorization of individuals into groups, relating to concepts such as privilege and power. Finally, the outer layer 'Unified Systems of Oppression' represents both the interaction of an individual with the outside world and the perception the outside world has of an individual. Drawing inspiration from Bešić's presentation, a new conceptualization of the interlocking elements of identity specific to teacher educators is depicted in Figure 2.

Figure 2 shows how differing identity filters for teacher educators may impact on their practice and the desired inclusive outcomes for teacher education. The quest for outcomes

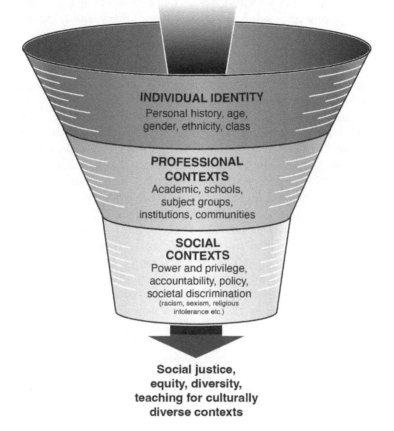

INDIVIDUAL IDENTITY
Personal history, age,
gender, ethnicity, class

**PROFESSIONAL
CONTEXTS**
Academic, schools,
subject groups,
institutions, communities

**SOCIAL
CONTEXTS**
Power and privilege,
accountability, policy,
societal discrimination
(racism, sexism, religious
intolerance etc.)

**Social justice,
equity, diversity,
teaching for culturally
diverse contexts**

FIGURE 2 *An identity filter for teacher education. Adapted from Bešić, 2020.*

for teacher education that embrace social justice, equity and diversity is the result of various identity contexts. This metaphorical representation highlights both the multifaceted nature of individual identity and the need to be attuned to societal perceptions. This speaks to the complex world of teacher educators, whose practice is inevitably framed by their own identity markers and whose work must engage with the perceptions and assumptions of the teachers and aspirant teachers with whom they interact.

The starting point is *individual identity*, located in the personal, comprising multiple identities related to past experience and societal perception. Self-reflection is a powerful tool in the examination of identity, as indicated by the plethora of studies from practicing teacher educators reflecting on their own practice. Teacher educators come to their practice having already had experience of schools as a student and, for many, as a teacher. The assumptions and beliefs developed during this apprentice of observation are not grounded in a knowledge of what it means to work with teachers. As Bullock (2009: 299) notes, in her practice, 'My experiences as a teacher candidate did not prepare me to be a teacher educator any more effectively than my experiences as a student prepared me to be a teacher.' Active self-reflection on the nature of the role and the many individual beliefs and influences that shape professional practice is, therefore, an important and necessary part of becoming a teacher educator.

Who we are will inevitably inform what we do, and the work of teacher educators is situated in multiple *professional contexts*, each with their own values and agendas. Simultaneous membership of numerous professional groups further complicates the identity of the teacher educator, who is often working across and between groups. As discussed in Chapter 3, opportunities for bespoke induction and targeted professional development may be sparse. Kosnik et al. (2015a) note the positive potential in establishing communities of teacher educators both within and across universities, a practice that could helpfully be expanded to include contexts in school and the wider community. The rise in digital connections in response to the Covid-19 pandemic highlights the opportunities for the creation of online communities, which may allow for some focused interaction across groups in different settings, which could serve to focus discussions and reflections around professional identity.

Finally, *societal contexts* highlight the influences of the outside world on teacher education, with professionals working within contexts that may be both restrictive and discriminatory. This can extend to matters of policy, both within institutions and at a national or international level. Teacher educators may not have the agency to influence such policy, but recognition of the extent to which identity and practice are influenced by external factors is an important part of becoming a self-assured professional.

Recognition of this process of filtration is important in unpacking the multiple levels of identity in the lives of teacher educators and the teachers with whom they work. To move away from imitation of previously experienced practices, Bullock (2009) advocates the power in listening to teacher candidates, acknowledging that their views and beliefs on teaching and learning may differ from those held personally. The teacher educator is also thus identified as a learner, developing their pedagogy of education in conjunction with and in response others. As Kosnik et al. (2015b: 214) summarize, 'Teachers of teaching need to simultaneously be learners of teaching in order to understand the complexity of learning to teach through student teachers' eyes.'

Time spent on teacher education courses addressing the complexity of individual, professional and socially situated identities can also help develop approaches to ensuring social justice and equity for the pupils with whom teachers work. There is a need for teacher educators to look both inward and outward, while recognizing 'who is missing in the room' (Harris and Leonardo, 2018: 20). Bei (2019) highlights the perpetual nature of the work: 'What must follow is daily commitment to become intersectionality-minded educators, constantly checking our own biases, working to dismantle our own deficit, majoritarian thinking as well as the wider cultures, structures and barriers that prevent true inclusion for all' (Bei, 2019, n.p.).

So how can such practices become embedded into teacher education programmes? An explicit engagement with a critical multiculturalism that includes exploration of critical race theory and cultural politics can encourage the challenging of preconceived ideas, assumptions and biases, developing critical knowledge about the realities of history (Fylkesnes, 2018). However, exposure does not necessitate engagement. As Vavrus (2010: 28) notes, 'Students who encounter critical histories of white supremacy and sexism … often deflect this information away from their identities in a manner that does not threaten stable status quo notions of themselves.' Utilization of such models as the identity filter depicted in Figure 2 may prove fruitful for personal, professional and group reflection, but productive and meaningful reflection cannot be assumed. It is important, particularly in the field of pre-service education, that skills of reflection are specifically taught through the framing of critical questions that seek to highlight the socially constructed assumptions that underpin identities.

Culturally Responsive Practice

Despite the increasingly diverse nature of student populations, there is a marked lack of demographic diversity in teacher education (Ellis, Souto-Manning and Turvey, 2019), characterized by the 'mono-cultural, mono-racial make-up of the teacher education professoriate' (Goodwin and Kosnik, 2013: 341) and an 'overwhelming presence of Whiteness' (Sleeter, 2001: 102). Although teacher education researchers use and give meaning to the term cultural diversity, it has been claimed that this usage is suggestive of the researchers' positionality (Fylkesnes, 2018). A lack of diversity is also reflected in the teaching population. For example, a study conducted by researchers at the Institute of Education, University College London (Tereshchenko, Mills and Bradbury, 2020) found that 46% of all schools in England had no Black, Asian and minority ethnic (BAME) teachers, and even in ethnically diverse schools, BAME teachers were under-represented in senior leadership teams. A similar picture is found in the United States, as noted by Gay (2013): 'In the United States teachers are predominately middle class, female, monolingual, and of European ancestry, while students are increasingly poor and linguistically, ethnically, racially, and culturally diverse' (Gay, 2013: 64).

Significantly, Goodwin et al.'s (2014) research reported teacher educators as feeling inadequately prepared for addressing diversity, with the less-experienced educators more attuned to diversity and multicultural issues than their more-experienced counterparts.

In advocating culturally responsive teaching, Gay (2013: 63) emphasizes the relevance of contextual specificity, highlighting how instructional practices should be 'shaped by the sociocultural characteristics of the settings in which they occur, and the populations for whom they are designed'. Such focus on situated practice is also evident in the use of multicultural autobiography (Leckie and Buser De, 2020) and autoethnography (Vavrus, 2010) as a reflective tool. Autoethnography serves to connect the autobiographical and personal to the cultural, political and social context, and through its use, 'identity formation can be linked to social phenomena rather than imagined as historically autonomous from political forces.' (Vavrus, 2010: 28). Vavrus (2010) describes how the undertaking of structured writing tasks alongside the critical exploration of autoethnographic narratives in workshops prompted teacher candidates to interrogate how the knowledge of their own personal history explored through the autoethnographic lens informed understanding of the formation of their respective teacher identity.

Working with teacher educators in the United States, Souto-Manning (2019) adopts a collaborative approach to tackling the obstacles to social justice in teacher education. Informed by the results of surveys and interviews conducted with university-based teacher educators, and specifically the emergent theme of a construction of student teaching in schools populated by intersectionally minoritized children of colour as 'problems', she gained entry to a state school to engage in weekly collaboration with a class teacher. Joined by other staff at the school, the group engaged in discussions, conceptually framed as Freirean culture circles. This collaborative reflection addressed the nuances of their professional and personal identities, impacting on the possibilities of future practice: 'This group of teachers relished the opportunity to critically read their worlds centring their perspectives as women of colour, positioning themselves agentively, and developing a professional collective committed to transformation' (Souto-Manning, 2019: 106).

Despite such empowering opportunities, the fact remains that in the United States (and elsewhere), the demographic of teacher education programmes does not reflect the diversity of the student population in schools. As Sleeter (2017: 155) notes, 'Changing who sits at the table is partly a hiring issue, but it is also a matter of who one collaborates with.' She highlights how teacher educators can broaden the range of 'voices at the table' through focused collaborations with local communities and schools, confronting inequities of race directly and, in so doing, encouraging critical reflections on identity and positionality.

Conclusion

The development of teacher educators' practice is inextricably linked to the development of their professional identity. In addressing what it means to be a teacher educator in a diverse educational world, the multiplicity of identity offers a lens for the exploration of the personal and the professional, informing both what teacher educators do and think. The practice of teaching is inherently social and often motivated by a desire to improve the outcomes of others – in short to make a difference. This intrinsic motivation is framed within political and societal contexts that often lie outside of the control of the individual. The resulting expression is cognitive and emotional, simultaneously outward looking and internally felt. As Davey (2013: 16) notes, professional identity 'may be publicly expressed, but it is quite privately located'.

It is vital that we acknowledge and learn from the intersectional nature of identity. In the broadest sense, intersectionality can be seen as a 'standpoint from which to view educational problems and possibilities, human limitations and liberations (Harris and Leonardo, 2018: 19). The adoption of a questioning stance informed by collaborative approaches and self-reflection promotes the 'daily commitment to become intersectionality-minded educators' (Bei, 2019), responding to the realities of cultural diversity.

CHAPTER FIVE

Social Identity and Collaborative Practices

Teacher educators are often working at the intersection between conflicting worlds (Olsen and Buchanan, 2017) in an increasingly marketized environment. Such experiences can be isolating, and in response, this chapter directly addresses the relevance of sustained collaboration both within and across contexts in the development of professional identity. It is important to encourage the continued exploration of new and innovative models of teacher education that embrace an expansive notion of practice, acknowledging the centrality of social relationships and the necessity of engaging with community-based knowledge. In so doing, teacher educators are encouraged to look outward from their specific professional context, developing the scope of their professional identity as they work alongside other educators across institutional and cultural boundaries.

Key Points

- The relevance of a social identity approach in examining teacher educator identity;

- how the professional identity formation of teacher educators is positively influenced by collaborative and partnership working;
- the importance of collaboration with communities in the identity development of socially just teacher educators.

Social Identity

Teacher educators work in a variety of contexts, often without formalized induction and training systems. The 'lonely enterprise' (Lorist and Swennen, 2016) of becoming a teacher educator can be an isolating experience, sitting counter to the often collaborative nature of education itself. Addressing social isolation, Haslam et al. (2016) note how the 'social identity approach' (Haslam, 2004; Haslam, Reicher and Platow, 2011) can help account for the effect that social group ties have on cognitions, emotions and behaviour. The social identity approach is rooted in two social psychological theories – social identity theory (Tajfel and Turner, 1979) and self-categorization theory (Turner et al., 1987): 'Fundamental to these theories is the idea that social group memberships furnish people with a distinctive sense of self arising from internalized social identities that entail ties to other ingroup members' (Haslam et al., 2016: 189).

In the social identity approach, the self is seen as fluid and context dependent, represented on both a personal and a collective level. Professional behaviours are governed by a sense of group membership or shared social identity as well as, if not more than, a sense of individualized self – the 'we' as opposed to the 'I' (Haslam et al., 2016). This inclusion in a group can have emotional benefits, and support between people who share a social identity has been shown to reduce levels of stress (van Dick and Haslam, 2012).

There is a growing body of research deploying the social identity approach for the analysis of teacher identity. For example, in their systematic review of the literature pertaining to middle and/or high school science teachers' identities, Rushton and Reiss (2020) adopt a social identity approach in their linking of an otherwise disparate literature base. However, despite its relevance, adoption of a social identity approach within teacher education research is surprisingly less common (Andreasen, Bjørndal and Kovač, 2019). With the diversity of identities at play in the world of teacher education, association with like-minded professionals can facilitate a sense of group membership. For university-based teacher educators, a sense of shared social identity may arise within departments where informal induction procedures and ongoing peer support can help promote a sense of collective belonging. Equally, participation in local communities of practice (Wenger, 2000) can aid identity development, particularly when intentionally formed and subject specific (Dinkelman, 2011), while engagement with self-study and practitioner-centred inquiry may serve to highlight contextual features at play in professional decision-making.

Involvement in such communities of practice is particularly significant for teacher educators working in schools. Developing a professional identity as a teacher educator in this context can be challenging as juggling the dual role of teacher and teacher educator is further problematized by the prevalence of traditional, hierarchical relationships between universities and schools (Ellis and McNicholl, 2015). Andreasen, Bjørndal and Kovač's (2019) study conducted with mentor teachers working with primary and lower-secondary teacher education partnered with two universities in Norway foregrounds the difficulties in developing effective and non-hierarchical relationships between mentors in schools and university partners, presenting the development of a teacher educator identity for mentor teachers as 'a complex interplay of the social processes found at one's own institution, personal dispositions, and the organization of the teacher education at the HE-institution'

(Andreasen, Bjørndal and Kovač, 2019: 288). Their findings showed that mentor teachers' identification with other teacher educators within their school had a positive impact on the development of a teacher educator identity. Inevitably, participation in such communities of practice with other teacher educators in the same school will affect the experience of the individual, with learning and identity formation becoming entwined (Lave and Wenger, 1991). However, such benefits are dependent on the self-categorization of mentor teachers in schools as teacher educators, which is not always apparent (Livingston, 2014). Even when collaborative practices are enacted, there is the potential for viewpoints to be limited by the specificity of context. From their research into the professional agency of Finnish university-based teacher educators, Hökkä, Eteläpelto and Rasku-Puttonen (2012) advocate the development of support structures for boundary crossing between subject groups, exploiting opportunities for common research efforts across departments. More broadly, Murray (2005) acknowledges the importance of coherent departmental induction to the identity development of new teacher educators, but warns of the dangers of parochialism and anecdotal approaches, advocating the provision for engagement with perspectives that extend beyond institutional settings.

Identity Formation through Collaboration

Collaboration between teacher educators via professional learning communities (PLCs) that extend beyond their specific context is therefore essential to the development of professional identities and collective agency. One example of such a community is the International Forum for Teacher Educator Development (InFo-TED) discussed in Chapter 3. The forum's aim to 'bring together people across the world to exchange research and practice related to teacher educators' professional development' (Kelchtermans, Smith and Vanderlinde, 2018: 129) emphasizes the centrality of collaboration, and the forum's conceptual framework (see Figure 1) provides a shared language for teacher educators across international and institutional borders to engage in collaborative research. This is apparent in the numerous collaborative ventures outlined in the forum's White Paper (InFo-TED, 2019) and in the provision of a Summer Academy in 2018, financed by European Commission (ERASMUS+) funding. The academy was held in Trondheim, Norway, and gathered teacher educators from around the world as part of the forum's intention to develop a knowledge base for the professional development of teacher educators (Czerniawski, Guberman and MacPhail, 2017). Auto-ethnographical reflections, vignettes and journals gathered by Kidd, McMahon and Viswarajan (2019) highlight the positive experience of engagement in the shared professional community offered by the week-long academy, 'The most valuable aspect of this was the opportunity to interact with peers from a wide range of professional backgrounds and contexts: the fact that the groups were internationally mixed made it all the more interesting' (Kidd, McMahon and Viswarajan, 2019: 42).

For author Ann McMahon, the impact of engagement with this community of practice resonated beyond the academy, foregrounding how such collaborations assisted with the complex nature of boundary crossing associated with a move into higher education from teaching: 'I have developed more confidence in my new role and an understanding of its overlapping complexities. I am aware of the journey I am on to developing a new professional identity that reflects the nature of higher education' (Kidd, McMahon and Viswarajan, 2019: 44).

In this instance, the opportunity to collaborate with and learn from other teacher educators across countries and contexts assisted with a growing awareness of what a higher education professional identity can look like.

Other collaborative ventures have focused on the development of future teacher educators. Kosnik et al. (2011) report on the Becoming Teacher Educators (BTE) initiative, a community group at Ontario Institute for Studies in Education at the University of Toronto in Canada. The group was specifically designed for doctoral students whose career goal is to become teacher educators. Voluntary monthly meetings between doctoral students and two professors provided a means for the exploration of the role and identity of teacher educators and included activities such as discussing scholarly articles, observing and interviewing teacher educators, hearing presentations by members of BTE on their research, discussing job applications and the differing university contexts, and providing feedback on research proposals and grant applications. Significantly, involvement in this group had a direct impact on professional identity development, with BTE members identifying 'several processes and critical incidents that contributed strongly to their emerging identities as teacher educators' (Kosnik et al., 2011: 357). This included the navigation of tensions arising from the enactment of multiple identities (doctoral student, classroom teacher, beginning teacher educator) and the emerging identity as a researcher, facilitated by the discussed readings and the delivery of critical presentations. Analysis of the impact of the BTE group highlights its key elements: 'its strengths as a community, the importance of shared leadership, the opportunity to develop knowledge of teacher education, the improvement of research skills, the influence on identity, and improvement in practices as beginning teacher educators' (Kosnik et al., 2011: 360).

Arising from collaboration between both peers and more knowledgeable others in Vygotskian terms, the BTE group provides a useful blueprint for identity development and practice in higher education institutions within and beyond the Canadian context.

Global North approaches to teacher education dominate teacher education programmes and research literature (Saavedra and Perez, 2018), but collaborative identity work is also evident in the Global South. For example, Widodo and Allamnakhrah (2020) report on the impact of a blended PLC on teacher educators' professional identity, involving 200 teacher educators from twenty Indonesian universities. Their case study of thirty teacher educators chronicles the formation of a PLC comprising workshops, peer observations, reflective dialogue and collective reflections over a three-year period. Participation in the PLC was found to assist the participants in 'shifting their professional identity from a curriculum deliverer to a curriculum maker' (Widodo and Allamnakhrah, 2020: 410), a practice that continued following the end of the original three-year period. Dahlström and Nyambe's (2014) case studies of Global South teacher education practices in Laos, Ethiopia and Namibia demonstrate how counter-hegemonic practices of critical pedagogy offer alternatives to the dominance of globalized neoliberal forces. In the exploration of identity development, the most notable feature is the opening up of site-based continuing professional development of beginner and veteran teachers, an initiative driven by The National Institute for Educational Development (NIED). This collaborative approach draws on local funds of knowledge held in schools and community-based centres to facilitate Continuing Professional Development activities locally. Combined with action research and critical practitioner inquiry based in schools, this bottom-up, participatory approach provides critical arenas for teachers and teacher educators to explore issues of identity, pedagogy and practice. It also provided the impetus for the development of a two-year induction and mentoring programme for beginner teachers by the NIED. Although there is nothing groundbreaking in the practice, it is empowering, and Dahlström and Nyambe (2014) emphasize its significance in response to previously experienced didacticism: 'While the content of the current program resemble the usual stuff in teacher education, this program provides an avenue for possible critical pedagogies in order to counteract the damage on new teachers by neoliberal pedagogies' (Dahlström and Nyambe, 2014: 103).

Identity in Partnership

The symbiotic relationship between universities, schools and other teacher education sites is central to the ongoing development of teacher educator identity. As Loughran and Menter (2019) observe, 'Quality teacher education is dependent on effective partnerships between universities and schools in order to create well-structured programs based on critical interrogation and research into pedagogical experiences and practices as a positive way of fostering development and change for the future' (Loughran and Menter, 2019: 226).

In England, the implementation of government Circular 9/92 for secondary education (DfE, 1992) brought the statutory requirement for higher education institutions to enter into formal partnership arrangements with schools. The publication of the Coalition Government's White Paper *The Importance of Teaching* in November 2010 (DfE, 2010) saw an increase in the proportion of time pre-service teachers spent in classrooms and heralded the introduction of School Direct, a training route that placed schools in the driving seat of both the selection and recruitment of aspirant teachers. Such changes in the power dynamics between schools and universities can challenge genuine collaborative practices. In seeking to redress this, Murtagh and Birchinall (2018) detail the development of communities of practice between University of Manchester and clusters of primary schools in the delivery of their Primary Postgraduate Certificate in Education programme. This school–university partnership was premised on school-based research, and their findings highlight the importance of trust in the development of relationships, as 'participants were increasingly able to share their experiences with each other in a safe environment' (Murtagh and Birchinall, 2018: 93). Participation in the project also led to a 're-imaging' of identities for both teachers and university participants. For school-based participants, the emergence of a researcher identity was apparent, while university-based participants found that involvement in the project led to a reassessment of their role in schools and a greater awareness of the diversity of the teacher role. Over time, the project elicited a collective sense of ownership: 'The key to developing school-university partnerships may lie in seeking opportunities for developing genuine models of collaboration where research-engaged teachers, university staff and trainee teachers are obliged to commit to a spirit of shared learning' (Murtagh and Birchinall, 2018: 94).

The re-imagining of traditional school and university partnerships as communities of practice, therefore, affords opportunities for shared identity development, although the pressures of time and the logistical tensions in managing both a teacher and researcher identity simultaneously are notable barriers.

Partnerships can also operate on an international scale. For example, Posti-Ahokas et al. (2021) report on a collaboration between the College of Education in Eritrea and Finnish universities. The study concerned the professional identities of Eritrean teacher educators and how these identities can be strengthened through collaborative professional practice. Participants attended 'Educators' Forums', a series of biweekly professional development seminars jointly facilitated by Eritrean and Finnish educators. Through engagement with participatory, learner-centred techniques, the attendees at the forums explored the research-based content of teacher educator identity, the quality of teaching and learning, and pedagogies for active learning. Analysis of session evaluations, individual interviews and drawings of teacher self-images by ten of the participants revealed that the provision of a space for discussion and reflection had helped with professional identity development, leading to clear visions among the participants of how they wanted to develop. In the creation of 'critical colleagueship', the partnerships with Finnish institutions proved to be highly beneficial, making international connections by providing exposure to an alternative education system through joint seminars, workshops, research and visits to Eritrea and

Finland: 'Research collaboration, especially when initiated from the South, can become a significant space for institutional learning and improvement and an opportunity to decolonise institutional partnerships' (Posti-Ahokas et al., 2021: 313).

A Mentor Identity

The relationship between pre-service teachers and their teacher educator mentors emphasizes the centrality of collaborative practice and the relevance of support in the development of professional identity. The role of mentors in schools in facilitating and encouraging the formation of the necessary connections between private sense making and public meaning is pivotal. Such relationships are also important in the development of teacher educators themselves. Izadinia (2014) identifies the relevance of both self-support and community support activities in the formation of the teacher educator identity, particularly at times of transition. Focusing on this transitional period, Brudvik, Gourneau and Tack's (2018) US-based study comprised interviews with seven former classroom teachers who had transitioned to teacher educators. Reference to mentorship and collaboration appeared in every interview, with reflections of positive mentors and collaborations described as swimming through the minds of the participants. Calling for more systematic professional collaboration, the authors recommend the formal provision of a mentor for new faculty members, emphasizing the reciprocal nature of such relationships as experienced staff 'benefit from new energy and new ideas' and novice staff 'benefit from the professional experience and a broader view of academia' (Brudvik, Gourneau and Tack, 2018: 17). The way in which mentoring can contribute to the development of such broader perspectives is also noted by Thornton (2014), who emphasizes the role of mentors as agents of change in schools, with the provision of spaces for reflection empowering institutional change.

While there is broad agreement that both the provision of mentorship and participation in the practice of mentoring are supportive of the development of professional identity, it must be recognized that such practices are situated in contested contexts. The 'enduring struggles' (Holland and Lave, 2001) of working within institutional settings will inevitably impact on the nature and experience of mentoring and can lead to tensions. Thornton (2014) identifies the culture of the school and/or district as the main barrier to mentors acting as change agents in their place of work. This institutional-level conflict is evident in the following reflection from a novice teacher in Brudvik, Gourneau and Tack's study on the nature of her relationship with her university departmental mentor: 'We also navigated tricky workplace scenarios together. I didn't feel supported by the administration but felt supported by her. Even though administration holds the winning card, at times, her support was much more important because of the close, personal level, and helpful feedback' (Brudvik, Gourneau and Tack, 2018: 12).

Such tensions are also apparent in schools. While the mediating role of the school mentor is vital in encouraging and supporting the identity development of pre-service teachers, the necessary judgmental element of the role can be problematic. This is echoed in the characterization of mentoring in England as 'vulnerable practice' (Lofthouse and Thomas, 2014; Hobson, 2016):

Mentoring of student teachers in their prospective workplaces is vulnerable practice. For example the desired outcomes of mentoring may become more narrowly defined by the stakeholders, who are pre-occupied by the demands to meet the performance targets for both pupil achievement and compliance with teacher standards. This is not to deny the importance of the quality of new teachers' classroom practice, but this technical view may lead participants in teacher education to overlook the complex, iterative and relatively fragile processes which underpin initial teacher development. (Lofthouse and Thomas, 2014: 215)

Mentoring encounters in the field of education are, therefore, situated in political, cultural and historical settings replete with conflicting demands and contrasting desired outcomes. This will inevitably impact on the development of professional identity, as 'taking part in contentious local practice shapes intimate identities in complex ways' (Holland and Lave, 2009: 3). This serves to further emphasize the importance of supportive collaborations, ensuring that both teachers and teacher educators are not left to navigate the complex and contested educational environments alone.

Community Collaborations

Engagement with local communities offers opportunities for the re-conceptualization of both the role and identity of teacher educators. As Murrell (2001: 4) states, 'Community teachers have a clear sense of their own cultural, political, and racial identities in relation to the children and families they hope to serve. This sense allows them to play a central role in the successful development and education of their students' (Murrell, 2001: 4).

There has long been an awareness of the need for educators to engage with the communities that are served by local schools, but the majority of research studies report on the preparation of pre-service teacher candidates rather than the long-term hiring of community-based teacher educators (Guillen and Zeichner, 2018). It is not uncommon for community-based expertise to feature in teacher education courses, particularly in North America, but respect for non-professional community-based knowledge is not always evident (Zeichner, Payne and Brayko, 2015).

There may not be formal recognition for the role of parents, youth workers and other community leaders, but the opportunities for collaboration and engagement are rich. For example, White (2019) outlines how in Australia the cultural knowledge of Aboriginal and Torres Strait Islander elders is essential to the preparation of culturally informed teachers. The specific requirement to demonstrate learning in two key areas features in the national professional teaching standards:

> Focus Area 1.4: Strategies for teaching Aboriginal and Torres Strait Islander Students
> Focus Area 2.4: Understand and respect Aboriginal and Torres Strait Islander people to promote reconciliation between Indigenous and non-Indigenous Australians. (The Australian Professional Standards for Teachers , 2011, cited in White, 2019: 202)

Similarly, Lees (2016) reports on a community–university partnership for teacher preparation with an urban Indigenous community organization in Chicago. Indigenous community partners from diverse tribal nations participated in the study, working as co-teacher educators to improve teacher preparation for Indigenous education. The partnership was between the Kateri Center of Chicago, an urban Indigenous community organization, and Loyola University's Teaching, Learning, and Leading with Schools and Communities, a field-based, teacher preparation programme, and featured a two-week 'Community Immersion' module in which each Kateri community partner was paired with two candidates to 'mentor and assist with their module projects and share their knowledges around Indigenous education' (Lees, 2016: 368). There was some frustration from the community mentors to the response from the teacher candidates in the short time and a suggestion that the community funds of knowledge were not fully embraced. As one mentor comments, 'Their awareness wasn't as great considering they talked to all of us and we know the community, they didn't use our knowledge' (Lees, 2016: 372). However, there was also a keen sense of the need for active involvement in supporting in-service teachers in their work with urban Indigenous children, filling the gap in such provisions at the national level. Lees (2016) calls for teacher preparation programmes to sanction change in Indigenous education: 'They must commit to decolonizing the institution and embrace community partners' active roles in fostering candidates' understandings around teaching Indigenous children' (Lees, 2016: 376).

Such changes highlight both the varied identities of teacher educators, embracing the knowledge and expertise of community-based mentors, and the need for teacher education itself to reconsider its identity. A redefining of the existing power structures in universities to give equal value to community knowledge has the potential to provide a richer and more authentic experience for pre-service and in-service teachers and for teacher educators.

Democratizing Teacher Education

> In our view, the preparation of teachers for a democratic society should be based on an epistemology that in itself is democratic and includes a respect for and interaction among practitioner, academic, and community-based knowledge. (Zeichner, Payne and Brayko, 2015: 124)

Zeichner, Payne and Brayko (2015) describe a 'critical time' for teacher education, with a need for the utilization of 'hybrid' spaces, where schools, universities and communities can work together to support teacher learning and identity development outside of traditional hierarchies. The emphasis is on non-hierarchical collaborative practice, with hybrid spaces offering new opportunities for the development of shared identity and practice. This is also evident in research conducted by Norton-Meier and Drake (2010). They sought to understand the interactions of pre-service teachers in the overlapping spaces provided by homes, universities, schools and communities. The analysis of their findings points to a conceptualization of a 'third space' that transcends the physicality of the academic setting, addressing key issues around the formation of a professional identity.

This focus on horizontal expertise and the learning that takes place in the spaces created across boundaries is important to the development of both teacher and teacher educator identities. The recognition of the significance of community knowledge to the development of teachers invites a reformulation of the approach to teacher education based on shared experience that is rooted in a commitment to social justice. As Zeichner, Payne and Brayko (2015) note, 'Neither schools nor universities can educate our nation's teachers alone and that even together, schools and universities cannot educate teachers well without accessing the expertise that exists in the communities that are supposed to be served by schools' (Zeichner, Payne and Brayko, 2015: 132).

Engagement in genuine collaborative approaches to teacher education that resist hierarchical structures and embrace knowledge and expertise across the boundaries of schools, universities and communities offers a means both for the re-evaluation of the teacher educator identity and a reassessment of whose knowledge counts in the pursuit of equitable education for all.

Conclusion

Back in 1986, Ducharme described the multiple identities of the teacher educator as including school person, scholar, researcher, methodologist, and 'visitor to a strange planet' (Ducharme, 1986: 1), the latter encompassing both the variance among students and the difficulties that teacher educators can experience on transition into higher education. These distinctions are still present today but could be helpfully extended to include the emotionally relational aspect of the role as teacher educators participate in such activities as mentoring, counselling and community liaison. Despite the many guises and differences in teacher educators across countries and contexts, there is also a sense of shared purpose. This sense of collective identity or belonging is reported by Davey (2013), whose research revealed teacher educators struggling to feel part of the various communities with which they interacted: 'It was the sense of "us" that was proving more problematic, fractured, dislocated, and in a state of flux – a consequence perhaps of their consciousness of working in the "spaces in between" professional communities rather than having a recognised or valued space *within* them' (Davey, 2013: 161).

His participants describe feeling comfortable with their own identities as teacher educators but less certain of the status of teacher education among the various professional communities (in schools and universities) with which they interacted.

Collaboration between teacher educators via PLCs that extend beyond their specific context can contribute, therefore, to feelings of collective identity and common purpose. Local, national and international collaborations are important in establishing connections across boundaries and borders, providing focused professional development that is bespoke to teacher educators. There is, however, also something powerful about inhabiting the 'spaces in between'. The position of teacher educators is unique in straddling the worlds of schools, higher education and communities, facilitating connections across contexts. As Zeichner, Payne and Brayko (2015) emphasize, there is strength in the utilization of 'hybrid' spaces, where schools, universities and communities can work together outside of traditional hierarchies. It is in these hinterlands that teacher educators can find a collective identity, united in the support of teacher learning irrespective of context.

CHAPTER SIX

Identity, Conflict and Innovation

Conflicting views and agendas characterize the world of education. Globally, an increasing emphasis on accountability and measures of effectiveness have resulted in the marketization and commodification of teaching (Ben-Peretz and Flores, 2018), while the presentation of teaching as a 'craft ... best learnt as an apprentice' (Gove, 2010) serves to de-professionalize the role of teacher educators, impacting directly on identity. This chapter addresses the nature of the teacher educator identity in an era of conflict and change, identifying points of tension and considering how the Covid-19 pandemic has necessitated the reassessment and redesign of existing identities and practices.

Key Points

- The impact of the de-professionalization of teacher educators on identity;
- conflict and tensions in the formation of the teacher educator identity;
- how teacher educators might work to normalize the inevitable experience of conflict as an integral part

of the teacher preparation process, supporting the formation of the teacher identity;

- teacher educator identity in an era of change, including the impact of the Covid-19 pandemic on the profession.

The De-professionalization of Teacher Educators

Globally, educational issues have become increasingly framed as 'problems that require policy solutions' (Skourdoumbis, 2017: 206). Educationalists find themselves working in a 'regime of assurance, standards and regulations' (Churchward and Willis, 2019: 260) where discourses of accountability and a perceived need for 'classroom-ready teachers' (TEMAG, 2014) dominate. In this 'labyrinth of performativity' (Ball, 2003: 220), improvement in teacher quality is seen as the solution to addressing structural inequalities in society, and teachers and teacher educators are held responsible for failure (Steadman and Ellis, 2021). Teachers and students are ' "responsibilised" for the quality and outcomes of education' (Torrance, 2018: 83), and teacher educators 'are often explicitly or implicitly held accountable for teacher quality and are frequently blamed when school students do not meet national or international expectations' (Cochran-Smith et al., 2020: 5), thus marginalizing the impact of other societal and contextual factors that lie beyond the classroom door. Discourses of accountability have altered the professional landscape in education and inevitably impact on how teachers and teacher educators come to define themselves and their success (Buchanan, 2015).

In this performative environment, debates around the identity of teacher educators and the nature of teacher education ensue, with contrasts drawn between the conceptualization of teachers as craftworkers or 'executive technicians' (Zeichner, 2012; Orchard and Winch, 2015), tasked with improving standardized test scores, and a broader view of teachers as long-term professionals and researchers. In many countries, reference to 'teacher education' has been replaced by 'teacher training'. This is notable in England where references to 'student teacher' had been replaced with 'trainee' in government publications by 2003. The notion of 'teacher training' with a focus on key skills differs from the values and principles that underpin 'teacher education', which has been described as 'a multidisciplinary and collaborative field of inquiry' (UCET, 2020). In England, the political discourses around teacher preparation continue to emphasize a perceived separation of theoretical instruction from a more practical application in schools, evident in the presentation of teaching by then Education Secretary Michael Gove in 2010: 'Teaching is a craft and it is best learnt as an apprentice observing a master craftsman or woman. Watching others, and being rigorously observed yourself as you develop, is the best route to acquiring mastery in the classroom' (Gove, 2010).

In addition, the introduction of Teachers' Standards in England (DfE, 2011) and elsewhere established a centralized baseline of expectations for the professional practice and conduct of teachers. This increased focus on the mastery of a set of skills and competences further developed a view of teacher professionalism 'heavily weighted' towards the management of behaviour (Evans, 2011). Parallels can be drawn between England and the United States, as noted by Cochran-Smith (2015: xii), who sees neoliberal perspectives in both countries as 'nearly imperceptible as ideology' and 'more likely understood as common sense'. This sense of tacit acceptance of policy is referenced by Ball (2013: 39), who, bemoaning the creation of a 'weary, wary and fearful' teaching workforce, calls for a move towards democratic professionalism as an antidote to the increasing neoliberal agenda, with an emphasis instead on 'collaborative, cooperative action between teachers and other educational stakeholders'.

A technicist framing of teachers impacts on the role and identity of those tasked with preparing newcomers to the profession, contributing to feelings of de-professionalization as the emphasis becomes more on the acquisition of key skills rather than the development of lifelong learners. As John Dewey warned in 1904, 'Immediate skill may be got at the cost of power to go on growing' (1904: 15). One outcome of this de-professionalization of teacher educators is an impact on agency. Caught within the mandates of national and local policy, teacher educators can find themselves acquiescing to practices that are not aligned to their own beliefs and values. Such experiences of de-professionalization are synonymous with a loss of autonomy and control over individual professional development. As Buchanan (2015: 704) comments, 'An individual's professional agency is reciprocally related to his or her professional identity.'

Reclaiming Professional Identity

One approach to reclaiming agency within an environment of de-professionalization is chronicled by Franklin Torrez and Haniford (2018), two teacher educators who undertook a collaborative self-study to explore their professional identities. The stimulus for the study came in the form of a mandatory three-day training course in their college of education at a research university in the south-western United States. Frustrated by the lack of agency in managing their own professional development, the two colleagues undertook a series of writing and discursive reflective tasks, resulting in the identification of themes (described as continua). One continuum is labelled 'agency vs acquiescence', with discussions initially centred on their feelings of professional marginalization in response to the training course. However, through their exploration, they come to see that acquiescence need not be seen as inaction. Although they felt the impact of the external mandates on their agency, they also chose not to give up, an active decision that incorporated accepting the current situation and expending energies instead in the areas of their professional life over which they had more control: 'The recursive process of self-study allowed us to move from feeling angry, marginalized and powerless to recognizing that even within deprofessionalization there is room for choice in our acquiescence, which has given us a new sense of agency' (Franklin Torrez and Haniford, 2018: 112).

A focus on self-study is well established in teacher education research, demonstrating agentic practice as teacher educators take the lead in analysing the complexities of their own profession. Introspective reflection invites interpretation and reinterpretation of beliefs and values, emphasizing the dynamic nature of professional identity.

In presenting the interplay between identity and agency, Beauchamp and Thomas (2011: 7) articulate how the active construction of teacher identity is inevitably combined with the imposition of identity 'stemming from societal or cultural conceptions of teachers'. The same can be said for teacher educators, whose identities will always be formed in response to societal and cultural discourses. Churchward and Willis (2019) discuss how unpacking competing discourses of teacher quality can aid the work of teacher educators. Drawing on Gee's distinctions between semantic 'discourses' and the larger social narratives of 'Discourses', their thematic literature review reveals six Discourses evident in the policy agenda of teacher quality:

> Three prominent Discourses, classroom readiness, standards, and effectiveness, were visible as each term was connected directly with the phrase 'quality', while three, responsibilisation, performativity and identity were obscured, that is they were implied, becoming evident after examining the agendas and beliefs given significance in the texts. (Churchward and Willis, 2019: 254)

Acknowledging the complexity of working in a policy environment with such competing policy agendas, they highlight how informed teacher educators can help students to navigate the various quality discourses and help empower teacher colleagues to 'move beyond the compliance cascade' (Churchward and Willis, 2019: 260).

The agency of teacher educators is also evident in their presentation as 'reformers' offered by Cochran-Smith et al. (2018). Their analysis details approaches to teacher education reform that are 'initiated, developed, and promoted by teacher educators themselves' (Cochran-Smith, Keefe and Carney, 2018: 572) and also highlights the conflicting and competing stances within the reformer identity. Focusing on teacher educators as reformers in relation to pre-service teacher preparation in the United States, they identify three broad approaches, referred to as entrepreneurial reform, managerial reform and democratic reform. In their analysis, entrepreneurial reformers are associated with new teacher education programmes, including those situated in what they identify as 'new graduate schools of education' (nGSEs), offering an approach to teacher education characterized by a 'deliberate move to disrupt and bypass university teacher education and leave behind business as usual' (Cochran-Smith, Keefe and Carney, 2018: 576). Entrepreneurial teacher reformers are situated within a broader context in the United States, where accountability and effective practice are central and university-based teacher education is presented as the 'problem' that needs to be fixed by relocating teacher preparation to nGSEs. The converse to this is the managerial reformers 'led by teacher education's old guard', with a focus on addressing the 'problem' of university teacher education through standardization, where the 'solution' is 'to hold teacher education accountable for impact and effectiveness using universal tools and assessments' (Cochran-Smith, Keefe and Carney, 2018: 580).

As noted by Ellis, Steadman and Trippestad (2019), this construction of the university-based teacher education system as the 'problem' is imbued in the discourses of the Global Education Reform Movement or GERM (Sahlberg, 2011, 2012). This 'neoliberal restructuring of public education systems' (Fuller and Stevenson, 2019: 3) is defined by Sahlberg as including increased standardization, a focus on core subjects/ knowledge (evidenced in international assessment surveys, such as PISA), the adoption of corporate management models and the growth of high stakes accountability. Cochran-Smith, Keefe and Carney (2018) argue that for their final group, the 'democratic reformers', it is the impact of such neoliberal education reform that is the 'problem' rather than university-based teacher education: 'Democratic reformers construct the "solution" to the problem – or the reform that is needed – as transformation of the work of teacher education, including resistance to the dominant accountability paradigm and an additive and democratic approach to education writ large' (Cochran-Smith, Keefe and Carney, 2018: 582).

For democratic reformers, social justice is key as they aim to interrogate the structures and systems of teacher education that are perceived to lead to educational inequity.

The analysis offered by Cochran-Smith, Keefe and Carney (2018) is context specific and, by their own admission, not designed as an evaluation or critique of the approaches of teacher educators. However, in terms of identity, it does provide interesting insight into the question of what kind of teacher educator is needed for today's world. The formulation of the three separate groups of 'reformers' emphasizes the competing and conflicting agendas present in global discourses of teacher education. But the positioning of teacher educators as agents of change rather than objects of reform also foregrounds the possibilities inherent in taking a stance, openly interrogating the conflicts and challenges that exist in local, national and global contexts. Through such interrogation, issues of professional identity are foregrounded and a sense of belonging can be cultivated.

Identity, Tensions and Conflict

Psycho-social conflict is intrinsic to becoming a member of an 'impossible profession' (Freud, 2001) and inherent in the

formation of the teacher educator identity. The education
environment itself is replete with conflicting discourses, and
teacher educators often experience conflict and tensions as
they transition from previous professional settings. Those
learning to teach can face tensions as they move between sites
of learning, encountering contrasting views and practices that
impact on the formation of their professional identity and
their agency. The ability to acknowledge and reflect on both
contextual and cognitive conflicts can impact positively on
the formation of professional identity, 'shaping and reshaping'
(Williams, 1976: 24) the self and encouraging the adoption of
an agentic stance.

The complexity of the education field, with a plethora of
policy actors involved in debates over teacher quality and
educational reforms, means that conflicts are unavoidable.
The articulation of the 'enduring struggles' (Holland and Lave,
2001) present in both the localized and broader landscapes
of teacher education are an important element in teacher
educator identity formation, inviting reflection that extends
beyond the self. Kelchtermans (2009: 270) emphasizes the
necessity of a contextualized approach to reflection 'in which
the particularities of one's working context are carefully taken
into account, whilst also being fundamentally questioned'. He
calls for teacher educators to make space for engagement in
'discomforting dialogues', addressing the moral, emotional
and political dimensions that characterize conceptualizations
of teaching and teacher education. This embracing of challenge
has the potential to impact directly on professional identity
and agency, highlighting conflicts and tensions in order to
acknowledge and better understand personally held beliefs.
Although teacher educators may find themselves constrained
by forces beyond their control, the collaborative articulation
and analysis of what can and cannot be achieved invites deep
reflection and a sense of empowerment. As Franklin Torrez
and Haniford (2018: 112) discovered through their joint
self-study, 'Learning to see the current context honestly and

making informed choices as to how to adjust one's response can open up new pathways of agency.'

Tension in the field of teacher education is perhaps most keenly felt at points of transition. As we have seen, many teacher educators come to the role via previous work as teachers, moving from first-order practitioners, working as schoolteachers in the first-order setting of the school, to second-order practitioners, working as teacher educators in the second-order setting of the university (Murray and Male, 2005). This foregrounds the tensions in reconciling the teacher identity with the process of becoming a teacher educator, highlighting the 'identity dissonance' (Warin and Muldoon, 2009) that can occur with the transition between professional roles. Boyd and Harris (2010) identify this 'teaching transfer' as problematic, highlighting how new teacher educators can see their credibility as a successful school teacher as both important and reassuring. Wishing to maintain this professional credibility with student teachers can impact on the development of an identity as a teacher educator, stalling the first-order to second-order transition. Equally, previous experience as a teacher brings with it beliefs about teaching and accepted practices. For the teacher educator, it is important to identify the extent to which these passions and practices are modelled with their students, remaining receptive to potential conflicts between personally held beliefs and the views and experiences of others. When working with newcomers to the profession, it is vital to provide opportunities and support for them to explore their developing teacher identity rather than promoting imitation.

As discussed in Chapter 3, professional development and induction can assist with the process of developing an identity as a teacher educator. Noting O'Brien and Furlong's (2015: 390) concern that for new teacher educators 'there is no discursive space for critical reflection, development or reshaping of identity', Amott (2018) addresses how the adoption of a narrative approach to professional development for neophyte teacher educators can assist with identification of their new role and professional identity. Her study utilizes a narrative life history approach, with both individual and group discussions providing the means for 'reflecting on reflection'. Although the narrative storytelling proved useful in activating a process of identification that enabled the participants to develop a more secure understanding of their professional identity as teacher educators, the practice is reliant both on the presence of a researcher and the availability of shared time. An individual approach to examining the process of transition and addressing tensions can be seen in the development of a teaching portfolio, as outlined by Hamilton (2018). She details how the development of a teaching portfolio provided both a systematic tool to capture evidence of practice and the primary source of data for analysis of the practice. The suggested template included the sections:

- Philosophy of teaching
- Planning and preparation for teaching
- Teaching effectiveness and performance
- Assessment and evaluation of student learning
- Professional development: past, present and future

Utilizing this structured, evidenced approach to reflection facilitated a level of deep personal and professional understanding, serving to highlight and address moments of tension and aid transition: 'My experience developing a teaching portfolio challenged my prior beliefs about teaching and learning. It helped with the formation of a teacher educator identity, where I began to understand and develop a philosophy of what it means to teach about teaching' (Hamilton, 2018: 93).

Such identity work is important for teacher educators. Reflecting on personally held beliefs not only aids the development of an identity as a teacher educator, but also allows for the identification and encouragement of differing stances from students and others already working in the field of education. Part of the role of a teacher educator is to encourage the development of a teacher identity in others, informed rather than restricted by the beliefs and experiences of the self.

Conflict in the pre-service teacher experience continues to be a richly researched area in the sociocultural field (see e.g. Smagorinsky et al., 2004; Ó Gallchóir, O'Flaherty and Hinchion, 2018). The necessity of working across differing locations can lead to the formation of inner doubts or 'critical conflicts' (Vasilyuk, 1988) that can leave individuals feeling vulnerable. Pre-service teachers find themselves caught in the 'dilemma situation' (Engeström, 1987) of simultaneously trying to satisfy the demands of their teacher education providers and placement schools. The challenge for teacher educators lies in normalizing the inevitable experience of conflict as an integral part of the formation of the teacher identity (Steadman, 2021). The foregrounding of uncertainty and emotion is important in guiding new teachers through processes of personal–professional change, with reflections situated in the political and cultural landscape. Investing time in discomforting dialogues (Kelchtermans, 2009), both with pre-service teachers and between teacher educators, is important in the development of identity, and the provision of spaces for habitual reflection can help promote agency in 'imagining alternative possibilities' (Reeves, 2018: 105) to restrictive regulations and policies.

Such practice is evident in many teacher education programmes. For example, Lassila et al. (2017) discuss the use of peer group mentoring sessions in Finland aimed at encouraging emotional and rational reflection. Nichols et al. (2017) suggest that teacher education programmes should centre mindfulness exercises, drawing links between emotional episodes and the development of professional teacher identities. A failure to address emotions can be limiting, as noted by Day and Leitch (2001): 'Often unacknowledged feelings of hurt, guilt, resentment, fear, injustice, and shame, for example, are common at the interface of the person of the teacher and his or her professional identity' (Day and Leitch, 2001: 403).

The facilitation of structured discussions around anticipated tensions, both in teacher preparation sites and in meetings with school-based mentors, can help alleviate the emotional vulnerability of those who find themselves caught between conflicting practices and values.

Teacher Educator Identity in an Era of Change

Teaching and learning in this digital era compel teacher educators to re-examine their professional identity. For most students coming to teacher education programmes, interactions with a range of technology are part of their daily existence (Avidov-Ungar and Forkosh-Baruch, 2018), with unfettered access to information and the ability to constantly adopt and adapt an online identity that can be shared with a diverse audience via social networking sites. This technological engagement does not necessarily equate to knowledge about how to use such tools in the process of teaching, and teacher educators are increasingly concerned with how to manage the creation and delivery of digital content for a twenty-first-century blended classroom (Dickenson and Sistek-Chandler, 2016). Whereas traditionally teacher education programmes have been housed in universities and schools deploying face-to-face teaching, the increased utilization of a blended approach to learning changes the dynamic, re-framing the relationship between the educator and the learner. Online practices enable the broader sharing of teaching and discussion, allowing teacher educators to work collaboratively across locations. In this shared space, power relations change as the previous physical boundaries between schools, universities and communities are removed.

The global Covid-19 pandemic presented teacher educators with significant challenges, as evident in the rapidly growing international literature base (see, for example, Kidd and Murray, 2020; la Velle et al., 2020; Scull et al., 2020; Darling-Hammond and Hyler, 2020). The loss of the practicum during periods of lockdown necessitated exploration of alternative pedagogical responses, with a relocating and re-positioning of student learning into online spaces. Such radical and rapid changes in practice inevitably impact on professional identity. The emotional intensity of the experience of responding to the Covid-19 crisis in a complex and uncertain context is evident in the accounts of the teacher education leaders interviewed by Ellis, Steadman and Mao (2020). Their research sought to assess whether changes made in response to the pandemic might be classed as innovations, re-centring the identity of teacher educators as innovators. Despite the emotionality, there was also a powerful sense of agency in the teacher educators' reflections – a sense of responsibility for the future of the teacher workforce, as the unprecedented context rewrote the norms of the educational landscape. The intensity of the work during the Covid-19 pandemic highlighted the unsustainability of the historical practices, and the data consistently revealed the adoption of an innovative stance. Analysis of the interviews consistently revealed a recognition and awareness among these leaders of their own agency and often an explicit desire not to return to pre-pandemic practices. Significantly, the necessity of a creative and rapid response to the crisis served to 'reprofessionalise' the leaders, freeing them from political constraint and allowing the space for focused, context-specific practices, evident in the reflection below:

> I felt that too long we as a sector we've been appeasing government and government policy making, always saying well we can live with it, we can manage it. And gradually, there's been this erosion of what we believe in, and it's I think it's time to stop and say, look, we've had enough of this. We're not going to have this anymore (Edward, Elsmere, Europe). (Ellis, Steadman and Mao, 2020: 568)

Although exhausting, the experience of enacting change during the pandemic was also empowering, with the innovator identity demonstrating how 'agency and identity are intertwined' (Buchanan, 2015: 705). The move online has opened up opportunities for greater inclusion and access to training, such as in British Columbia where there are remote communities, many with large Indigenous populations, who could benefit from an online or blended approach to teacher education (Hill et al., 2020).

Conclusion

As teacher educators continue to work in contested and conflicting spaces, identity remains a powerful lens through which to explore their professional selves. As Jenlink (2006) writes, 'Teacher educators must engage in a pedagogy of identity that critically examines the consequences that dominant discourses and practices have had in the creation of their own lives and the lives of their students' (Jenlink, 2006: 13). Jenlink's representation of identity as a 'palimpsest' effectively captures the way in which teacher educator's identities are formed and re-formed in response to personal, cultural and political forces.

The Covid-19 pandemic placed significant and sustained pressure on teacher educators. But it also provided a glimpse of a conception of identity and practice that is not rooted in historical norms. As usual methods of working were rendered obsolete, teacher educators were quick to react and remodel, adopting innovative responses to the unfolding crisis. The closure of schools and universities brought the immediate need for teacher educators to address issues of access, participation and engagement for their students (Scull et al., 2020), but also revealed heightened opportunities for collaborative work. Some teacher preparation programmes reported strengthened collaboration with different departments within universities (Darling-Hammond and Hyler, 2020) and the movement online provided opportunities for broader collaborations, including the connection of pre-service teachers with a wider range of teacher-mentors (Kidd and Murray, 2020). In times of crisis, teacher educators began to feel empowered to change practices both to address the immediate situation and for the future. There was, for some, a sharpening of their identity as teacher educators and a recognition of how the cultivation of a global mindset (Goodwin, 2020) that reaches beyond local contentious practice can come to shape the field of teacher education. It is important that the innovator identity of teacher educators continues to be embraced, re-framing the teacher educator identity as agents of change, rather than the objects of global reform and accountability measures.

Conclusion

This book has explored the importance of identity in developing an understanding of what it is to be a teacher educator in a complex and contested educational world. Starting with exploration of the messy and recursive process of learning to teach, the identity formation of the teacher educator has been scrutinized through consideration of the nature of practice, the importance of collaboration and partnerships and the inevitable presence of conflict and tensions. Professional identity has been presented as neither singular nor static, produced over time and in relation to others, as apparent in the definition adopted by Holland et al. (1998): 'We take identity to be a central means by which selves, and the sets of actions they organise, form and re-form over personal lifetimes and in the histories of social collectivities' (Holland et al., 1998: 270).

The dynamic nature of the teacher educator identity in times of change has been examined, including how the response to the Covid-19 pandemic has seen teacher educators adopting an identity as innovators.

We have seen how identities are also rooted in 'situated participation in explicit local conflict' (Holland and Lave, 2001: 5). For teacher educators, local conflict is often manifested by the paradoxical situation of having to enact external policies that run counter to personally held beliefs and historically experienced encounters. Internationally, educational reforms have created conditions whereby increased accountability and regulation have come to define the work of teacher educators, with an emphasis on performativity resulting in a 'sense of being constantly judged in different ways, by different means, according to different criteria, through different agents and agencies' (Ball, 2003: 220). It is in the experience of this struggle that identities become vulnerable. As Alsup states, 'The danger of a life lived amid paradox is the loss of a sense of self' (Alsup, 2019: 132). It is hard to maintain a sense of professional autonomy while juggling the needs of the self and other.

It is perhaps this amalgamation of personal sense making, uncertainty and vulnerability that explains the overwhelming interest in identity as a keyword in teacher education. For many teacher educators, there is a sense of purpose and a commitment to the role that transcends professional practice. As Franklin Torrez and Haniford (2018: 107) state, 'We consider ourselves teacher educators. This is more than a job, it is an identity.' Understanding this identity and its impact on practice is rooted in awareness of the self. Indeed, Kelchtermans (2009) goes as far as to dismiss identity as a useful term in favour of *self-understanding*: 'The term refers to both the understanding one has of one's "self" at a certain moment in time (product), as well as to the fact that this product results from an ongoing process of making sense of one's experiences and their impact on the "self"' (Kelchtermans, 2009: 261).

As teacher educators strive to know '" how to be", "how to act" and "how to understand" their work and their place in society' (Sachs, 2003: 135), the fusion of the personal and the professional spotlights the multiple selves at play, as past experiences and professional relationships inform the development of practice in situated and contentious landscapes.

Given this emphasis on self-awareness, it is not surprising that there should be an overwhelming methodological focus on self-study in identity research. Since 1993, when the Self-Study of Teacher Education Practices (S-STEP) was granted status as a Special Interest Group at the American Educational Research Association, there has been a rise in this research methodology, as evidenced by such publications as the *International Handbook of Self-Study of Teaching and Teacher Education Practices* (Loughran et al., 2004) and *Self-Study Research Methodologies for Teacher Educators* (Lassonde, Galman and Kosnik, 2009). Many of the projects examine personal moments of transition, often between a role as school teacher and teacher educator, and invariably include reference to how the process has informed knowledge of professional identity. For example, Williams and Ritter (2010) cite how inclusion in the self-study community of practice aided self-understanding. The methodology proved insightful, highlighting well-documented struggles: 'We discovered that becoming teacher educators represents an ongoing process fraught with competing and constantly changing tensions' (Williams and Ritter, 2010: 90). Personal discoveries of this nature are seen repeatedly in the expansive literature, undoubtedly contributing to the professional development of individuals but not always addressing the 'nagging question of "So what?"' (Kosnik et al., 2015b: 215). Back in 2007, Zeichner highlighted the need to connect the self-studies of teacher educators to the mainstream of teacher education research in order to influence policymakers and other teacher education practitioners (Zeichner, 2007). Similarly, Loughran (2010) asserts that while the narratives that dominate the self-studies of teacher educators are helpful, there is also a need to move beyond the stories. He states that for teacher educators, 'It is the learning derived from their researching of their practice that leads to the production of new knowledge of teacher education practices' (Loughran, 2010: 225). This learning builds on the work of others, making the connections advocated by Zeichner. While it is important to embrace individual reflection and self-awareness, it is also necessary for the identity of teacher educators to be taken seriously by those who sit outside of the profession. Bringing discussions of identity to the policy table requires an emphasis on its influence in shaping educational outcomes, moving beyond studies of the self to consider how pedagogy and practice informs the work of teachers and, ultimately, the performance of students in classrooms.

For teacher educators, identity is a keyword in teacher education. It speaks to notions of the personal and the professional, highlighting what it is to become and be a teacher educator. Identity is also a defining keyword of modern society, with the rise in identity politics emphasizing the power of collective group identities. However, the nuances of the teacher educator identity are not foregrounded in educational policy. Instead, globally, there is evidence of an increasingly narrow and technocratic view of teacher education that centralizes control and restricts the professional autonomy of teacher educators. Policy framed around effectiveness with an emphasis on issues of accountability and responsibility restricts the development of a dynamic identity grounded in the personal and enacted in a variety of contexts and in response to the needs of the individual. The need to embrace the necessary variance in identity is acknowledged by Brunila and Rossi (2018): 'We find that it is crucial to find a way to talk about identity politics and human subjectivity as sites of constant negotiation and agency without a fixed or foundational notion of subject or identity, especially in training teachers and researchers of education' (Brunila and Rossi, 2018: 294).

Teacher educators are a heterogeneous group, and the acknowledgement and embodiment of a universal teacher educator identity that applies across contexts is neither helpful nor possible. Those working with teachers (both as they enter the profession and throughout their careers) are drawn from a multiplicity of backgrounds and can face a variety of challenges as they transition between professional roles. There are typical stories to be told of the figured worlds that teacher educators inhabit. But as Gee (2014: 89) points out, what can be taken as typical 'varies between context and by people's social and cultural group'. But there is also a richness in this diversity, with opportunities for shared working across spaces. Collaboration between teacher educators via professional learning communities (in person and online) that extend beyond their specific context can contribute to feelings of collective identity and common purpose.

In the introduction to his book *Keywords: A Vocabulary of Culture and Society*, Raymond Williams observes that 'the most active problems of meaning are always primarily embedded in actual relationships' (Williams, 1976: 22). This book has shown how unpacking the 'problems of meaning' in the identity of teacher educators can be helpfully addressed through collaborative practices, offering opportunities for the development of professional identity through shared reflection and the joint creation of innovative ways of working. However, such work is not without its challenges. Working across boundaries requires a shift in professional identities as the contextual norms of working are challenged. The identification of teacher education as a 'policy problem' (Cochran-Smith, 2005: 3) highlights how notions of partnership are inevitably influenced by political agendas and can result in hierarchical systems that are counter to 'a two-way model of reciprocity' (Sachs, 2003: 6). For example, Mutton (2016) notes how teacher education policy in the UK has resulted in an approach to partnership focused on logistics and auditable outcomes. He emphasizes the need for shared conceptualizations across partnerships around the nature of teachers' professional knowledge and calls for engagement with the complexity of partnership working that is masked by the 'comfortable language' of bureaucracy (Mutton, 2016: 216). Despite these issues, collaboration between teacher educators across and within contexts provides opportunities for shared reflection on how best to support the development of culturally aware professionals equipped with the adaptive expertise to survive within a demanding profession (Steadman, 2018). Embracing the contributions of teacher educators in schools, universities and the community at large has the potential to enact a more democratic approach to teacher education (Zeichner, Payne and Brayko, 2015; Payne and Zeichner, 2017), inviting a reconceptualization of their role and identity.

REFERENCES

Akkerman, S., and Meijer, P. (2011). A Dialogical Approach to Conceptualizing Teacher Identity. *Teaching and Teacher Education*, 27, 308–19. doi:10.1016/j.tate.2010.08.013.

Alsup, J. (2006). *Teacher Identity Discourses – Negotiating Personal and Professional Spaces*. New York: Routledge.

Alsup, J. (2019). *Millennial Teacher Identity Discourses: Balancing Self and Other*. New York: Routledge.

Amott, P. (2018). Identification – A Process of Self-Knowing Realised within Narrative Practices for Teacher Educators during Times of Transition. *Professional Development in Education*, 44(4), 476–91. doi:10.1080/19415257.2017.1381638.

Andreasen, J. K., Bjørndal, C. R. P., and Kovač, V. B. (2019). Being a Teacher and Teacher Educator: The Antecedents of Teacher Educator Identity among Mentor Teachers. *Teaching and Teacher Education*, 85, 281–91. doi:10.1016/j.tate.2019.05.011.

Avidov-Ungar, O., and Forkosh-Baruch, A. (2018). Professional Identity of Teacher Educators in the Digital Era in Light of Demands of Pedagogical Innovation. *Teaching and Teacher Education*, 73, 183–91. doi:10.1016/j.tate.2018.03.017.

Ball, S. (2003). The Teacher's Soul and the Terrors of Performativity. *Journal of Education Policy*, 18(2), 215–28. doi:10.1080/026809 3022000043065.

Ball, S. (2013). *Policy Paper – Education, Justice and Democracy: The Struggle over Ignorance and Opportunity*. London: The Centre for Labour and Social Studies.

Ball, L. D., and Forzani, F. M. (2009). The Work of Teaching and the Challenge for Teacher Education. *Journal of Teacher Education*, 60(5), 497–511. doi:10.1177/0022487109348479.

Bateson, G., Jackson, D., Haley, J., and Weakland, J. (1956). Toward a Theory of Schizophrenia. *Behavioral Science*, 1(4), 251–4. doi:10.1002/bs.3830010402.

Beach, K. (1999). Consequential Transitions: A Sociocultural Expedition beyond Transfer in Education. *Review of Research in Education*, 24(1), 101–39. doi.org/10.3102/00917 32X024001101.

Beauchamp, C., and Thomas, L. (2009). Understanding Teacher Identity: An Overview of Issues in the Literature and Implications for Teacher Education. *Cambridge Journal of Education*, 39(2), 175–89. doi:10.1080/03057640902902252.

Beauchamp, C., and Thomas, L. (2011). New Teachers' Identity Shifts at the Boundary of Teacher Education and Initial Practice. *International Journal of Educational Research*, 50(1), 6–13. doi:10.1016/j.ijer.2011.04.003.

Bei, Z. (2019). Intersectionality & Inclusion. *Inclusion Now 54*. Available at https://www.allfie.org.uk/news/inclusion-now/ inclusion-now-54/intersectionality-inclusion/. Accessed 22 October 2022.

Beijaard, D. (2019). Teacher Learning as Identity Learning: Models, Practices, and Topics. *Teachers and Teaching*, 25(1), 1–6. doi:10.1 080/13540602.2019.1542871.

Beijaard, D., Meijer, P. C., and Verloop, N. (2004). Reconsidering Research on Teachers' Professional Identity. *Teaching and Teacher Education*, 20(2), 107–28. doi:10.1016/j. tate.2003.07.001.

Beijaard, D., and Meijer, P. C. (2017). Developing the Personal and Professional in Making a Teacher Identity. In J. Clandinin and J. Husu (Eds), *The SAGE Handbook of Research on Teacher Education* (Vol. 1, 177–92). London: Sage.

Ben-Peretz, M., and Flores, M. (2018). Tensions and Paradoxes in Teaching: Implications for Teacher Education. *European Journal of Teacher Education*, 41(2), 202–13. doi:10.1080/02619768.20 18.1431216.

Berliner, D. C. (1988). The Development of Expertise in Pedagogy. Charles W. Hunt Memorial Lecture, Presented at the Annual Meeting of the American Association of Colleges for Teacher Education, New Orleans.

Berry, A. (2016). Teacher Educators' Professional Learning: A Necessary Case of 'on Your Own'? In B. De Wever, R. Vanderlinde, M. Tuytens and A. Aelterman (Eds), *Professional Learning in Education – Challenges for Teacher Educators, Teachers and Student Teachers* (39–56). Gent: Academia Press.

Berry, A., Depaepe, F., and van Driel, J. (2016). Pedagogical Content Knowledge in Teacher Education. In J. Loughran and M. L. Hamilton (Eds), *International Handbook of Teacher Education* (347–86). London: Springer.

Bešić, E. (2020). Intersectionality: A Pathway towards Inclusive Education? *Prospects*, 49, 111–22. doi:10.1007/s11125-020-09461-6.

Biesta, G., Priestley, M., and Robinson, S. (2015). The Role of Beliefs in Teacher Agency. *Teachers and Teaching*, 21(6), 624–40. doi:10.1080/13540602.2015.1044325.

Bourdieu, P. (1991). *Language and Symbolic Power*. Cambridge: Harvard University Press.

Boyd, P., and Harris, K. (2010). Becoming a University Lecturer in Teacher Education: Expert School Teachers Reconstructing Their Pedagogy and Identity. *Professional Development in Education*, 36(1–2), 9–24. doi:10.1080/19415250903454767.

Britzman, D. P. (2003). *Practice Makes Practice – A Critical Study of Learning to Teach* (revised edition). Albany: State University of New York.

Britzman, D. P. (2009). *The Very Thought of Education: Psychoanalysis and the Impossible Professions*. New York: SUNY Press.

Brudvik, L., Gourneau, B., and Tack, D. (2018). Examining Identity of Novice Teacher Educators. *National Forum of Teacher Education Journal*, 28(3), 1–20.

Brunetti, G. J., and Marston, S. H. (2018). A Trajectory of Teacher Development in Early and Mid-Career. *Teachers and Teaching*, 24(8), 874–92. doi:10.1080/13540602.2018.1490260.

Brunila, K., and Rossi, L. M. (2018). Identity Politics, the Ethos of Vulnerability, and Education. *Educational Philosophy and Theory*, 50(3), 287–98. doi:10.1080/00131857.2017.1343115.

Buchanan, R. (2015). Teacher Identity and Agency in an Era of Accountability. *Teachers and Teaching*, 21(6), 700–19. doi:10.1080/13540602.2015.1044329.

Buchanan, R., and Olsen, B. (2018). *Teacher Identity in the Current Teacher Education Landscape*. In P. Schutz, J. Hong and D. Cross Francis (Eds), *Research on Teacher Identity* (195–205). Cham: Springer.

Bullock, S. (2009). Learning to Think Like a Teacher Educator: Making the Substantive and Syntactic Structures of Teaching

Explicit through Self-Study. *Teachers and Teaching: Theory and Practice*, 15(2), 291–304. doi:10.1080/13540600902875357.

Burn, K., Hagger, H., and Mutton, T. (2015). *Beginning Teachers' Learning: Making Experience Count*. St Albans: Critical Publishing.

Chua, A. (2018). *Political Tribes: Group Instinct and the Fate of Nations*. London: Bloomsbury.

Churchward, P., and Willis, J. (2019). The Pursuit of Teacher Quality: Identifying Some of the Multiple Discourses of Quality that Impact the Work of Teacher Educators. *Asia-Pacific Journal of Teacher Education*, 47(3), 251–64. doi:10.1080/13598 66X.2018.1555792.

Clarke, M. (2009). The Ethico-politics of Teacher Identity. *Educational Philosophy and Theory*, 41(2), 185–200. doi:10.1111/j.1469-5812.2008.00420.x.

Cochran-Smith, M. (2005). The New Teacher Education: For Better or for Worse? *Educational Researcher*, 34(7), 3–17. doi.org/10.31 02/0013189X034007003.

Cochran-Smith, M. (2015). Foreword. In Teacher Education Group (Ed.), *Teacher Education in Times of Change* (x-xvi). Bristol: Policy Press.

Cochran-Smith, M., and Lytle, S. (1999). Relationships of Knowledge and Practice: Teacher Learning in Communities. In G. Griffin (Ed.), *Review of Research in Education* (Vol. 24, 249–305). Washington, DC: American Educational Research Association.

Cochran-Smith, M., Cannady, M., Mceachern, K. P., Piazza, P., Power, C., and Ryan, A. (2011). Teachers' Education, Teaching Practice, and Retention: A Cross-Genre Review of Recent Research. *Journal of Education*, 191(2), 19–31. doi:10.1177/002205741119100205.

Cochran-Smith, M., Keefe, E., and Carney, M. (2018). Teacher Educators as Reformers: Competing Agendas. *European Journal of Teacher Education*, 41(5), 572–90. doi:10.1080/02619768.20 18.1523391.

Cochran-Smith, M., Grudnoff, L., Orland-Barak, L., and Smith, K. (2020). Educating Teacher Educators: International Perspectives. *The New Educator*, 16(1), 5–24. doi:10.1080/1547 688X.2019.1670309.

Collier, M. J., and Thomas, M. (1988). Cultural Identity: An Interpretive Perspective. In Y. Y. Kim and W. B. Gudykunst (Eds), *Theories in Intercultural Communication* (99–120). Newbury Park, CA: Sage.

Columbia Law School. (2017). Kimberlé Crenshaw on Intersectionality, More than Two Decades Later. Available at https://www.law.columbia.edu/news/archive/kimberle-crens haw-intersectionality-more-two-decades-later. Accessed 22 October 2022.

Combahee River Collective. (1977). *The Combahee River Collective Statement*. Mexico City: Gato-Negro.

Connelly, F. M., and Clandinin, D. J. (1999). *Shaping a Professional Identity: Stories of Education Practice*. London: Althouse Press.

Crawford, K. (2017). Conclusion. In P. M. Bamber and J. C. Moore (Eds), *Teacher Education in Challenging Times: Lessons for Professionalism, Partnership and Practice* (197–205). Oxon: Routledge.

Crawley, J. (2010). *In at the Deep End – a Survival Guide to Teachers in Post Compulsory Education* (2nd ed.). Abingdon: Routledge.

Crawley, J. (2013). 'Endless Patience and a Strong Belief in What Makes a Good Teacher': Teacher Educators in Post-Compulsory Education in England and Their Professional Situation. *Research in Post-Compulsory Education*, 18(4), 336–47. doi:10.1080/1359 6748.2013.847153.

Crenshaw, K. (1989). Demarginalizing the Intersection of Race and Sex: A Black Feminist Critique of Antidiscrimination Doctrine, Feminist Theory and Antiracist Politics. *University of Chicago Legal Forum*, 1, Article 8. Available at http://chicagounbound. uchicago.edu/uclf/vol1989/iss1/8. Accessed 22 October 2022.

Czerniawski, G. (2018). *Teacher Educators in the Twenty-First Century: Identity, Knowledge and Research*. St Albans: Critical Publishing Ltd.

Czerniawski, G., Guberman, A., and MacPhail, A. (2017). The Professional Developmental Needs of Higher Education-Based Teacher Educators: An International Comparative Needs Analysis. *European Journal of Teacher Education*, 40(1), 127–40. doi:10.1080/02619768.2016.1246528.

Czerniawski, G., Gray, D., MacPhail, A., Bain, Y., Conway, P., and Guberman, A. (2018). The Professional Learning Needs and Priorities of Higher-Education Based Teacher Educators in England, Ireland and Scotland. *Journal of Education for Teaching*, 44(2), 133–48. doi:10.1080/02607476.2017.1422590.

Dahlström, L., and Nyambe, J. (2014). Case Studies of Teacher Education Forces in the Global South: Pedagogical Possibilities When the Main Door Is Closed. *Journal for Critical Education Policy Studies*, 12(2), 74–111.

Darling-Hammond, L., and Hyler, M. E. (2020). Preparing Educators for the Time of COVID … and Beyond. *European Journal of Teacher Education*, 43(4), 457–65. doi:10.1080/02619 768.2020.1816961.

Davey, R. (2013). *The Professional Identity of Teacher Educators: Career on the Cusp?* London: Routledge.

Day, C., and Leitch, R. (2001). Teachers' and Teacher Educators' Lives: The Role of Emotion. *Teaching and Teacher Education*, 17(2001), 403–15. doi:10.1016/S0742-051X(01)00003-8.

Day, C., Kington, A., Stobart, G., and Sammons, P. (2006). The Personal and Professional Selves of Teachers: Stable and Unstable Identities. *British Educational Research Journal*, 32(4), 601–16. doi:10.1080/01411920600775316.

Deng, L., Zhu, G., Li, G., Xu, Z., Rutter, A., and Rivera, H. (2017). Student Teachers' Emotions, Dilemmas, and Professional Identity Formation Amid the Teaching Practicums. *Asia-Pacific Education Researcher*, 27(6), 441–53. doi:10.1007/s40299-018-0404-3.

Dewey, J. (1904). The Relation of Theory to Practice in Education. In C. A. McMurry (Ed.), *The Third Yearbook of the National Society for the Scientific Study of Education* (9–30). Chicago: University of Chicago Press.

DfE. (1992). Circular 9/92 Initial Teacher Training (Secondary Phase). London: DfE.

DfE. (2010). *The Importance of Teaching*. London: DfE.

DfE. (2011). *First Report of the Independent Review of Teachers' Standards*. London: DfE.

DfE. (2019a). *ITT Core Content Framework*. London: DfE. Available at https://assets.publishing.service.gov.uk/government/ uploads/system/uploads/attachment_data/file/974307/ITT_core _content_framework_.pdf. Accessed 22 October 2022.

DfE. (2019b). *Early Career Framework*. London: DfE. Available at https://assets.publishing.service.gov.uk/government/uploads/sys

tem/uploads/attachment_data/file/978358/Early-Career_Frame
work_April_2021.pdf. Accessed 22 October 2022.

Dickenson, P., and Sistek-Chandler, C. (2016). Blending Digital
Content in Teacher Education Programs. In J. Keengwe and G.
Onchwari (Eds), *Handbook of Research on Active Learning
and the Flipped Classroom Model in the Digital Age* (286–308).
Hershey, PA: IGI Global.

Dinkelman, T. (2002). Towards a Theory of Teachers Becoming
Teacher Educators. Paper presented at the Annual Meeting of the
American Educational Research Association, New Orleans, LA,
April 1–5, 2002.

Dinkelman, T. (2011). Forming a Teacher Educator Identity:
Uncertain Standards, Practice and Relationships. *Journal of
Education for Teaching*, 37(3), 309–23. doi:10.1080/02607476.2
011.588020.

Ducharme, E. R. (1986). *Teacher Educators: What Do We Know?*
ERIC Digest 15. Washington, DC: ERIC Clearing House on
Teacher Education.

Ducharme, E. (1993). *The Lives of Teacher Educators*.
New York: Teachers College.

Edwards, A. (2015). Recognising and Realising Teachers'
Professional Agency. *Teachers and Teaching*, 21(6), 779–84.
doi:10.1080/13540602.2015.1044333.

Ellis, V., and McNicholl, J. (2015). *Transforming Teacher
Education: Reconfiguring the Academic Work*.
London: Bloomsbury Academic.

Ellis, V., Souto-Manning, M., and Turvey, K. (2019). Innovation in
Teacher Education: Towards a Critical Re-Examination. *Journal
of Education for Teaching*, 45(1), 2–14. doi:10.1080/02607476.2
019.1550602.

Ellis, V., Steadman, S., and Trippestad, T. A. (2019). Teacher
Education and the GERM: Policy Entrepreneurship, Disruptive
Innovation and the Rhetorics of Reform. *Educational Review*,
71(1), 101–21. doi:10.1080/00131911.2019.1522040.

Ellis, V., Steadman, S., and Mao, Q. (2020). 'Come to a Screeching
Halt': Can Change in Teacher Education during the COVID-19
Pandemic Be Seen as Innovation? *European Journal of Teacher
Education*, 43(4), 559–72. doi:10.1080/02619768.2020.1821186.

Ellis, V., Mansell, W., and Steadman, S. (2021). A New Political
Economy of Teacher Development: England's Teaching and

Leadership Innovation Fund. *Journal of Education Policy*, 36(5), 605–23. doi:10.1080/02680939.2020.1717001.

Engeström, Y. (1987). *Learning by Expanding: An Activity-Theoretical Approach to Developmental Research.* Helsinki: Orienta-Konsultit.

Erickson, E. (1959). Identity and the Life Cycle. *Psychological Issues*, 1, 1–171.

European Commission. (2013). *Supporting Teacher Educators.* Brussels: EC.

Evans, L. (2002). *Reflective Practice in Educational Research: Developing Advanced Skills.* London: Continuum.

Evans, L. (2008). Professionalism, Professionality and the Development of Education Professionals. *British Journal of Educational Studies*, 56(1), 20–38. doi:10.1111/j.1467-8527.2007.00392.x.

Evans, L. (2011). The 'Shape' of Teacher Professionalism in England: Professional Standards, Performance Management, Professional Development and the Changes Proposed in the 2010 White Paper. *British Educational Research Journal*, 37(5), 851–70. doi:10.1080/01411926.2011.607231.

Evetts, J. (2008). The Management of Professionalism. In S. Gewirtz, P. Mahony, I. Hextall, and A. Cribb (Eds), *Changing Teacher Professionalism: International Trends, Challenges and Ways Forward* (19–30). Hoboken, NJ: Routledge.

Falk, B. (2006). A Conversation with Lee Shulman – Signature Pedagogies for Teacher Education: Defining Our Practices and Rethinking Our Preparation. *New Educator*, 2, 73–82.

Feiman-Nemser, S. (2001). Helping Novices Learn to Teach: Lessons from an Exemplary Support Teacher. *Journal of Teacher Education*, 52(1), 17–30. doi:10.1177/0022487101052001003.

Flores, M. A. (2020). Feeling Like a Student but Thinking Like a Teacher: A Study of the Development of Professional Identity in Initial Teacher Education. *Journal of Education for Teaching*, 46(2), 145–58. doi:10.1080/02607476.2020.1724659.

Flores, M. A., and Day, C. (2006). Contexts Which Shape and Reshape New Teachers' Identities: A Multi-perspective Study. *Teaching and Teacher Education*, 22(2), 219–32. doi:10.1016/j.tate.2005.09.002.

Franklin Torrez, C., and Haniford, L. (2018). Understanding Our Identities as Teacher Educators in an Era of

Deprofessionalization. In D. Garbett and A. Ovens (Eds), *Pushing Boundaries and Crossing Borders: Self-Study as a Means for Researching Pedagogy* (107–14). UK: S-STEP.

Freud, S. (1937). Analysis Terminable and Interminable. *International Journal of Psycho-Analysis*, 18, 373–405.

Freud, S. (2001). *The Complete Psychological Works of Sigmund Freud, Volume 6: The Psychopathology of Everyday Life* (J. Strachley, Ed.). London: Vintage Classics (original work published 1901).

Fuller, K., and Stevenson, S. (2019). Global Education Reform: Understanding the Movement. *Educational Review*, 71(1), 1–4. doi:10.1080/00131911.2019.1532718.

Furlong, J., and Maynard, T. (1995). *Mentoring Student Teachers: The Growth of Professional Knowledge*. London: Routledge.

Fylkesnes, S. (2018). Whiteness in Teacher Education Research Discourses: A Review of the Use and Meaning Making of the Term Cultural Diversity. *Teaching and Teacher Education*, 71, 24–33. doi:10.1016/j.tate.2017.12.005.

Garza, A. (2019). Identity Politics: Friend or Foe? Available at https://belonging.berkeley.edu/identity-politics-friend-or-foe#footnote1_bylmhjd. Accessed 22 October 2022.

Gatti, L. (2016). *Towards a Framework of Resources for Learning to Teach: Rethinking US Teacher Preparation*. New York: Palgrave Macmillan.

Gay, G. (2013). Teaching to and through Cultural Diversity. *Curriculum Inquiry*, 43(1), 48–70. doi:10.1111/curi.12002.

Gee, J. P. (2000). Identity as an Analytic Lens for Research in Education. *Review of Research in Education*, 25, 99–125.

Gee, J. P. (2014). *An Introduction to Discourse Analysis – Theory and Method*. New York: Routledge.

Geijsel, F., and Meijers, F. (2005). Identity Learning: The Core Process of Educational Change. *Educational Studies*, 31(4), 419–30. doi:10.1080/03055690500237488.

Goodwin, A. L. (2020). Globalization, Global Mindsets and Teacher Education. *Action in Teacher Education*, 42(1), 6–18. doi:10.1080/01626620.2019.1700848.

Goodwin, A. L., and Kosnik, C. (2013). Quality Teacher Educators = Quality Teachers? Conceptualizing Essential

Domains of Knowledge for Those Who Teach Teachers. *Teacher Development*, 17(3), 334–46. doi:10.1080/13664530.2013.813766.

Goodwin, A. L., Smith, L., Souto-Manning, M., Cheruvu, R., Tan, M. Y., Reed, R., and Taveras, L. (2014). What Should Teacher Educators Know and Be Able to Do? Perspectives From Practicing Teacher Educators. *Journal of Teacher Education*, 65(4), 284–302. doi:10.1177/0022487114535266.

GOV.UK. (2021). Initial Teacher Training (ITT) Market Review Report. Available at https://assets.publishing.service.gov.uk/gov ernment/uploads/system/uploads/attachment_data/file/999621/ITT_market_review_report.pdf. Accessed 22 October 2022.

Gove, M. (2010). Secretary of State for Education Address – National College Annual Conference. Available at https://www.gov.uk/government/speeches/michael-gove-to-the-national-coll ege-annual-conference-birmingham. Accessed 22 October 2022.

Gove, M. (2018). A New National Consensus? Building a Union Which Endures. Speech by Rt Hon Michael Gove MP for Policy Exchange, 21 May 2018. Available at https://policyexchange.org.uk/wp-content/uploads/2018/05/A-New-National-Consensus.pdf. Accessed 22 October 2022.

Griffiths, V., Thompson, S., and Hryniewicz, L. (2014). Landmarks in the Professional and Academic Development of Mid-Career Teacher Educators. *European Journal of Teacher Education*, 37(1), 74–90. doi:10.1080/02619768.2013.825241.

Grossman, P. (1990). *The Making of a Teacher*. New York: Teachers College Press.

Grossman, P., Smagorinsky, P., and Valencia, S. W. (1999). Appropriating Tools for Teaching English: A Theoretical Framework for Research on Learning to Teach. *American Journal of Education*, 108(1), 1–29. doi:10.1086/444230.

Grossman, P., Hammerness, K., and McDonald, M. (2009). Redefining Teaching, Re-Imagining Teacher Education. *Teachers and Teaching*, 15(2), 273–89. doi:10.1080/13540600902875340.

Guillen, L., and Zeichner, K. (2018). A University-Community Partnership in Teacher Education from the Perspectives of Community-Based Teacher Educators. *Journal of Teacher Education*, 69(2), 140–53. doi:10.1177/0022487117751133.

Hamilton, M. (2018). Bridging the Gap from Teacher to Teacher Educator: The Role of a Teaching Portfolio. *Studying Teacher Education*, 14(1), 88–102. doi:10.1080/17425964.2017.1414041.

Hargreaves, A. (2000). Four Ages of Professionalism and Professional Learning. *Teachers and Teaching*, 6, 151–82. doi:10.1080/713698714.

Harris, A., and Leonardo, Z. (2018). Intersectionality, Race-Gender Subordination, and Education. *Review of Research in Education*, 42(1), 1–27. doi:10.3102/0091732X18759071.

Haslam, S. A. (2004). *Psychology in Organizations*. London: Sage.

Haslam, S. A., Reicher, S. D., and Platow, M. J. (2011). *The New Psychology of Leadership: Identity, Influence and Power*. New York: Psychology Press.

Haslam, S. A., Peters, K., Steffens, N. K., and Reicher, S. D. (2016). *5R Manual*. Brisbane: Social Identity and Groups Network, University of Queensland.

Hill, C., Rosehart, P., St. Helene, J., and Sadhra, S. (2020). What Kind of Educator Does the World Need Today? Reimagining Teacher Education in Post-Pandemic Canada. *Journal of Education for Teaching*, 46(4), 565–75. doi:10.1080/02607476.2020.1797439.

Hiralaal, A. (2018). Exploring My Role Modelling as a Teacher Educator: A Self-Study. *South African Journal of Higher Education*, 32(6), 619–34. doi:10.20853/32-6-3001.

Hobson, A. J. (2016). Judgementoring and How to Avert It: Introducing ONSIDE Mentoring for Beginning Teachers. *International Journal of Mentoring and Coaching in Education*, 5(2), 87–110. doi:10.1108/IJMCE-03-2016-0024.

Hökkä, P., Eteläpelto, A., and Rasku-Puttonen, H. (2012). The Professional Agency of Teacher Educators Amid Academic Discourses. *Journal of Education for Teaching*, 38(1), 83–102. doi:10.1080/02607476.2012.643659.

Holland, D., and Lave, J. (Eds) (2001). *History in Person: Enduring Struggles, Contentious Practice, Intimate Identities*. Santa Fe: School of American Research Press.

Holland D. and Lave, J. (2009). Social Practice Theory and the Historical Production of Persons. *Actio: An International Journal of Human Activity Theory*, 2, 1–15.

Holland, D., Lachoitte, W., Skinner, D., and Cain, C. (1998). *Identity and Agency in Cultural Worlds*. Cambridge, MA: Harvard University Press.

Hong, J., Day, C., and Green, B. (2018). The Construction of Early Career Teachers' Identities: Coping or Managing? *Teacher*

Development, 22(2), 249–66. doi:10.1080/13664530.2017.140 3367.

Hoyle, E. (1975). Professionality, Professionalism and Control in Teaching. In V. Houghton et al. (Eds), *Management in Education: The Management of Organisations and Individuals* (314–20). London: Ward Lock Educational (in association with Open University Press).

InFo-TED (2019). The Importance of Teacher Educators: Professional Development Imperatives (White Paper). Available at https://info-ted.eu/wp-content/uploads/2019/10/InFo-TED-White-Paper.pdf. Accessed 22 October 2022.

Izadinia, M. (2013). A Review of Research on Student Teachers' Professional Identity. *British Educational Research Journal*, 39, 694–713. doi:10.1080/01411926.2012.679614.

Izadinia, M. (2014). Teacher Educators' Identity: A Review of Literature. *European Journal of Teacher Education*, 37(4), 426–41. doi:10.1080/02619768.2014.947025.

Jenlink, P. (2006). Learning Our Identity as Teacher: Teacher Identity as Palimpsest. *Teacher Education and Practice*, 19(2), 1–19.

Jesse, D. (2016, June 19). University of Michigan Education School Dean Stepping Down. Detroit Free Press. Available at http://www.freep.com/story/news/local/michigan/2016/06/18/deborah-loewenberg-ball-michigan/86034340/. Accessed 22 October 2022.

Jóhannsdóttir, T. (2010). Deviations from the Conventional: Contradictions as Sources of Change in Teacher Education. In V. Ellis, A. Edwards, and P. Smagorinsky (Eds), *Cultural-Historical Perspectives on Teacher Education and Development* (302–35). Oxon: Routledge.

Kelchtermans, G. (2009). Who I Am in How I Teach Is the Message: Self-Understanding, Vulnerability and Reflection. *Teachers and Teaching: Theory and Practice*, 15(2), 257–72. doi:10.1080/13540600902875332.

Kelchtermans, G., Smith, K., and Vanderlinde, R. (2018). Towards an 'International Forum for Teacher Educator Development': An Agenda for Research and Action. *European Journal of Teacher Education*, 41(1), 120–34. doi:10.1080/02619768.2017.1372743.

Kidd, W., McMahon, A., and Viswarajan, S. (2019). Developing a Pan-European Approach to Teacher Educators. *Research in Teacher Education*, 9(2), 39–45. doi:10.15123/uel.88z7v.

Kidd, W., and Murray, J. (2020). The Covid-19 Pandemic and Its Effects on Teacher Education in England: How Teacher Educators Moved Practicum Learning Online. *European Journal of Teacher Education*, 43(4), 542–58. doi:10.1080/02619768.20 20.1820480.

Kirabo, S. (2018). Why Criticisms of Identity Politics Sound Ridiculous to Me [blog post, 1 July 2018] Open Democracy. Available at https://www.opendemocracy.net/en/transformat ion/why-criticisms-of-identity-politics-sound-ridiculous-to-me/. Accessed 22 October 2022.

Knight, R. (2021). What Are the Signature Pedagogies of Teacher Education? [blog post, 13 August 2021] University of Nottingham. Available at https://blogs.nottingham.ac.uk/prim aryeducationnetwork/2021/08/13/what-are-the-signature-ped agogies-of-teacher-education/. Accessed 22 October 2022.

Korthagen, F. (2016). Pedagogy of Teacher Education. In J. Loughran and M. Hamilton (Eds), *The International Handbook of Teacher Education* (310–46). Dordrecht: Springer Press.

Kosnik, C., Cleovoulou, Y., Fletcher, T., Harris, T., McGlynn-Stewart, M., and Beck, C. (2011). Becoming Teacher Educators: An Innovative Approach to Teacher Educator Preparation. *Journal of Education for Teaching*, 3(3), 351–63. doi:10.1080/02607476.20 11.588027.

Kosnik, C., Menna, L., Dharamshi, P., Miyata, C., Cleovoulou, Y., and Beck, C. (2015a). Four Spheres of Knowledge Required: An International Study of the Professional Development of Literacy/ English Teacher Educators. *Journal of Education for Teaching*, 41(1), 52–77. doi:10.1080/02607476.2014.992634.

Kosnik, C., Miyata, C., Cleovoulou, Y., Fletcher, T., and Menna, L. (2015b). The Education of Teacher Educators. In T. Falkenberg (Ed.), *Handbook of Canadian Research in Initial Teacher Education* (207–24). Ottawa, ON: Canadian Association for Teacher Education.

Koster, B., and Dengerink, J. J. (2008). Professional Standards for Teacher Educators: How to Deal with Complexity Ownership and Function Experience from the Netherlands. *European Journal of Teacher Education*, 31(2), 135–49. doi:10.1080/02619760802000115.

Kumar, R. (2018). How Identity Politics Has Divided the Left: An Interview with Asad Haider. *The Intercept* [blog post, 27

May 2018]. Available at https://theintercept.com/2018/05/27/ identity-politics-book-asad-haider/. Accessed 22 October 2022.

Lampert, M. (2010). Learning Teaching in, from, and for Practice: What Do We Mean? *Journal of Teacher Education*, 61(1–2), 21–34. doi:10.1177/0022487109347321.

Lassila, E. T., Jokikokko, K., Uitto, M., and Estola, E. (2017). The Challenges to Discussing Emotionally Loaded Stories in Finnish Teacher Education. *European Journal of Teacher Education*, 40(3), 379–93. doi:10.1080/02619768.2017.1315401.

Lassonde, C., Galman, S., and Kosnik, C. (2009). *Self-Study Research Methodologies for Teacher Educators*. Rotterdam: Sense Publishers.

la Velle, L., Newman, S., Montgomery, C., and Hyatt, D. (2020). Initial Teacher Education in England and the Covid-19 Pandemic: Challenges and Opportunities. *Journal of Education for Teaching*, 46(4), 596–608, doi:10.1080/02607476.2020.180 3051.

Lave, J., and Wenger, E. (1991). *Situated Learning Legitimate Peripheral Participation*. New York: Cambridge University Press.

Leckie, A., and Buser De, M. (2020). The Power of an Intersectionality Framework in Teacher Education. *Journal for Multicultural Education*, 14(1), 117–27. doi:10.1108/ JME-07-2019-0059.

Lees, A. (2016). Roles of Urban Indigenous Community Members in Collaborative Field-Based Teacher Preparation. *Journal of Teacher Education*, 67(5), 363–78. doi:10.1177/0022487116668018.

Lemov, D. (2010). *Teach Like a Champion*. Hoboken, NJ: Jossey-Bass.

Livingston, K. (2014). Teacher Educators: Hidden Professionals? *European Journal of Education*, 49(2), 218–32. doi:10.1111/ ejed.12074.

Livingston, K., and Shiach, L. (2013). *Teaching Scotland's Future, Mentoring Pilot Partnership Project: Final Report. Project Report*. Livingston, UK: Education Scotland.

Lofthouse, R. M., and Thomas, U. (2014). Mentoring Student Teachers; a Vulnerable Workplace Learning Practice. *International Journal of Mentoring and Coaching in Education*, 3(3), 201–18. doi:10.1108/IJMCE-03-2014-0010.

Lorist, P., and Swennen, A. (Eds) (2016). *Life and Work of Teacher Educators*. Netherlands: Hogeschool Utrecht.

Lortie, D. (1975). *Schoolteacher: A Sociological Study*. Chicago: University of Chicago Press.

Loughran, J. (2006). *Developing a Pedagogy of Teacher Education: Understanding Teaching and Learning about Teaching*. London: Routledge.

Loughran, J. (2010). Seeking Knowledge for Teaching Teaching: Moving beyond Stories. *Studying Teacher Education*, 6(3), 221–6. doi:10.1080/17425964.2010.518490.

Loughran, J. (2011). On Becoming a Teacher Educator. *Journal of Education for Teaching*, 37(3), 279–91. doi:10.1080/02607476.2011.588016.

Loughran, J. J., Hamilton, M. L., LaBoskey, V. K., and Russell, T. (Eds) (2004). *International Handbook of Self-Study of Teaching and Teacher Education Practices*. Dordrecht: Springer.

Loughran, J. J., Mulhall, P., and Berry, A. (2008). Exploring Pedagogical Content Knowledge in Science Teacher Education: A Case Study. *International Journal of Science Education*, 30(10), 1301–20.

Loughran, J., and Menter, I. (2019). The Essence of Being a Teacher Educator and Why It Matters. *Asia-Pacific Journal of Teacher Education*, 47(3), 216–29. doi:10.1080/13598 66x.2019.1575946.

Lunenberg, M., and Hamilton, M. L. (2008). Threading a Golden Chain: An Attempt to Find Our Identities as Teacher Educators. *Teacher Education Quarterly*, 35(1), 185–205.

Lunenberg, M., Korthagen, F., and Zwart, R. (2011). Self-Study Research and the Development of Teacher Educators' Professional Identities. *European Educational Research Journal*, 10(3), 407–20. doi:10.2304/eerj.2011.10.3.407.

Lunenberg, M., Dengerink, J., and Korthagen, K. (2014). *The Professional Teacher Educator: Roles, Behaviour, and Professional Development of Teacher Educators*. Rotterdam: Sense Publishers.

McIntyre, J., Youens, B., and Stevenson, H. (2017). Silenced Voices: The Disappearance of the University and the Student Teacher in Teacher Education Policy Discourse in England. *Research Papers in Education*, 34(2), 153–68. doi:10.1080/02671 522.2017.1402084.

Mead, G. J. (2015). *Mind, Self and Society (1934): The Definitive Edition*. Chicago: University of Chicago Press.

Meeus, W., Cools, W., and Placklé, I. (2018). Teacher Educators Developing Professional Roles: Frictions between Current and Optimal Practices. *European Journal of Teacher Education*, 41(1), 15–31. doi:10.1080/02619768.2017.1393515.

Meijers, F., and Wardekker, W. L. (2003). Career Learning in a Changing World: The Role of Emotions. *International Journal for the Advancement of Counselling*, 24(3), 149–67.

Menter, I. (2018). Defining Teachers' Professional Knowledge: The Interaction of Global and National Influences. *Education and Self Development*, 13(1), 32–42. doi:10.26907/esd13.1.04.

Mewborn, D., and Tyminski, A. (2006). Lortie's Apprenticeship of Observation Revisited. *For the Learning of Mathematics*, 26(3), 30–2.

Mitchell, B., and Joseph, S. (2021). Teacher Educators in the Trinidad and Tobago Context: Perspectives from the Field. *Caribbean Curriculum*, 28, 180–200.

Mockler, N. (2013). Teacher Professional Learning in a Neoliberal Age: Audit, Professionalism and Identity. *Australian Journal of Teacher Education*, 38(10), 35–47. doi:10.14221/ajte.2013v38n10.8.

Murray, J. (2005). Re-addressing the Priorities: New Teacher Educators and Induction into Higher Education. *European Journal of Teacher Education*, 28(1), 67–85. doi:10.1080/02619760500040108.

Murray, J., and Male, T. (2005). Becoming a Teacher Educator: Evidence from the Field. *Teaching and Teacher Education*, 21, 125–42. doi:10.1016/j.tate.2004.12.006.

Murray, J., Czerniawski, G., and Barber, P. (2011). Teacher Educators' Identities and Work in England at the Beginning of the Second Decade of the Twenty-First Century. *Journal of Education for Teaching*, 37(3), 261–77. doi:10.1080/02607476.2011.588014.

Murray, J., Czerniawski, G., and Kidd, W. (n.d.). *Teacher Educators' Identities*. Available at https://info-ted.eu/identities/. Accessed 22 October 2022.

Murrell, P. (2001). *The Community Teacher*. New York: Teachers College Press.

Murtagh, L., and Birchinall, E. (2018). Developing Communities of Practice in School-University Partnerships. *Teacher Education Advancement Network Journal*, 10(1), 85–95.

Mutton, T. (2016). Partnership in Teacher Education. In The Teacher Education Group (Ed.), *Teacher Education in Times of Change* (201–16). Bristol: Policy Press.

Nguyen, H., and Loughland, T. (2018). Pre-service Teachers' Construction of Professional Identity through Peer Collaboration during Professional Experience: A Case Study in Australia. *Teaching Education*, 29(1), 81–97. doi:10.1080/10476210.2017.1353965.

Nias, J. (1986). *Teacher Socialisation – The Individual in the System*. New York: Hyperion Books.

Nias, J. (1989). *Primary Teachers Talking*. London: Routledge.

Nias, J. (1996). Thinking about Feeling: The Emotions in Teaching. *Cambridge Journal of Education*, 26(3), 293–306. doi:10.1080/0305764960260301.

Nichols, S., Schutz, P., Rodgers, K., and Bilica, K. (2017). Early Career Teachers' Emotion and Emerging Teacher Identities. *Teachers and Teaching*, 23(4), 406–21. doi:10.1080/13540602.2016.1211099.

Norton-Meier, L., and Drake, C. (2010). When Third Space Is More than the Library. In V. Ellis, A. Edwards, and P. Smagorinsky (Eds), *Cultural-Historical Perspectives on Teacher Education and Development*. Oxon: Routledge.

Nuttall, J., Brennan, M., Zipin, L., Tuinamuana, K., and Cameron, L. (2013). Lost in Production: The Erasure of the Teacher Educator in Australian University Job Advertisements. *Journal of Education for Teaching*, 39(3), 329–43. doi:10.1080/02607476.2013.799849.

O'Brien, M., and Furlong, C. (2015). Continuities and Discontinuities in the Life Histories of Teacher Educators in Changing Times. *Irish Educational Studies*, 34(4), 379–94. doi:10.1080/03323315.2015.1128349.

OED Online. (2021). 'identity, n.'. https://www.oed.com/oed2/00111224. Accessed 13 February 2022.

Ó Gallchóir, C., O'Flaherty, J., and Hinchion, C. (2018). Identity Development: What I Notice about Myself as a Teacher. *European Journal of Teacher Education*, 41(2), 138–56. doi:10.1080/02619768.2017.1416087.

Oliver, T. (2018). Here's a Better Way to Think about Identity Politics. *The Conversation*. Available at https://theconversation. com/heres-a-better-way-to-think-about-identity-politics-84144. Accessed 22 October 2022.

Olsen, B. (2012). Identity Theory, Teacher Education, and Diversity. *Encyclopaedia of Diversity in Education*, 1, 1123–6.

Olsen, B. (2016). *Teaching for Success: Developing Your Teacher Identity in Today's Classroom*. NY: Routledge.

Olsen, B., and Buchanan, R. (2017). Everyone Wants You to Do Everything: Investigating the Professional Identity Development of Teacher Educators. *Teacher Education Quarterly*, 44(1), 9–34.

Orchard, J., and Winch, C. (2015). *IMPACT 22: What Training Do Teachers Need? Why Theory Is Necessary to Good Teaching*. London: Philosophy of Education Society of Great Britain.

Palmer, P. (1998). *Courage to Teach: Exploring the Inner Landscape of a Teacher's Life*. San Francisco, CA: Jossey-Bass.

Payne, K. A., and Zeichner, K. (2017). Multiple Voices and Participants in Teacher Education. In J. Clandinin and J. Husu (Eds), *The SAGE Handbook of Research on Teacher Education* (1101–16). London: Sage.

Peterman, F. (2017). Identity Making at the Intersections of Teacher and Subject Matter Expertise. In D. J. Clandinin and J. Husu (Eds), *The SAGE Handbook of Research on Teacher Education* (193–209). London: Sage.

Philip, T. M., Souto-Manning, M., Anderson, L., Horn, I., Carter Andrews, D. J., Stillman, J., and Varghese, M. (2018). Making Justice Peripheral by Constructing Practice as 'Core': How the Increasing Prominence of Core Practices Challenges Teacher Education. *Journal of Teacher Education*, 70(3), 251–64. doi:10.1177/0022487118798324.

Pillen, M., Beijaard, D., and den Brok, P. (2013). Tensions in Beginning Teachers' Professional Identity Development, Accompanying Feelings and Coping Strategies. *European Journal of Teacher Education*, 36(3), 240–60. doi:10.1080/02619768.20 12.696192.

Posti-Ahokas, H., Idriss, K., Hassan, M., and Isotalo, S. (2021). Collaborative Professional Practice for Strengthening Teacher Educator Identities in Eritrea. *Journal of Education for Teaching*, 48(3), 300–15. doi:10.1080/02607476.2021.1994838.

Pugach, M., Gomez-Najarro, J., and Matewos, A. (2019). A Review of Identity in Research on Social Justice in Teacher Education: What Role for Intersectionality? *Journal of Teacher Education*, 70(3), 206–18. doi:10.1177/0022487118760567.

Reeves, J. (2018). Teacher Identity Work in Neoliberal Schooling Spaces. *Teaching and Teacher Education*, 72, 98–106. doi:10.1016/j.tate.2018.03.002.

Ritter, J. K. (2007). Forging a Pedagogy of Teacher Education: The Challenges of Moving from Classroom Teacher to Teacher Educator. *Studying Teacher Education*, 3(1), 5–22. doi:10.1080/17425960701279776.

Rodgers, C. R., and Scott, K. H. (2008). The Development of the Personal Self and Professional Identity in Learning to Teach. In M. Cochran-Smith, S. Feiman-Nemser, D. J. McIntyre, and K. E. Demers (Eds), *Handbook of Research on Teacher Education* (732–55). New York: Routledge.

Rushton, E., and Reiss, M. J. (2020). Middle and High School Science Teacher Identity Considered through the Lens of the Social Identity Approach: A Systematic Review of the Literature. *Studies in Science Education*, 57(2), 141–203. doi:10.1080/0305 7267.2020.1799621.

Saavedra, C. M., and Pérez, M. S. (2018). Global South Approaches to Bilingual and Early Childhood Teacher Education: Disrupting Global North Neoliberalism. *Policy Futures in Education*, 16(6), 749–63. doi:10.1177/1478210317751271.

Saber, N. (2004). From Heaven to Reality through Crisis: Novice Teachers as Migrants. *Teaching and Teacher Education*, 20, 145–61. doi:10.1016/j.tate.2003.09.007.

Sachs, J. (2003). *The Activist Teaching Profession*. Buckingham: Open University Press.

Sachs, J. (2005). Teacher Education and the Development of Professional Identity: Learning to Be a Teacher. In P. Denicolo and M. Kompf (Eds), *Connecting Policy and Practice: Challenges for Teaching and Learning in Schools and Universities* (5–21). Oxford: Routledge.

Sachs, J. (2016). Teacher Professionalism: Why Are We Still Talking about It? *Teachers and Teaching*, 22(4), 413–25. doi:10.1080/135 40602.2015.1082732.

Sahlberg, P. (2011). *Finnish Lessons: What Can the World Learn from Educational Change in Finland?* New York: Teachers College Press.

Sahlberg, P. (2012). How GERM Is Infecting Schools around the World? Available at https://pasisahlberg.com/text-test/. Accessed 22 October 2022.

Schön, D. A. (1987). *Educating the Reflective Practitioner.* San Francisco: Jossey-Bass.

Scull, J.,Phillips, M., Sharma, U., and Garnier, K. (2020). Innovations in Teacher Education at the Time of COVID19: An Australian Perspective. *Journal of Education for Teaching*, 46(4), 497–506. doi:10.1080/ 02607476.2020.1802701.

Shulman, L. (1987). Knowledge and Teaching: Foundations of the New Reform. *Harvard Educational Review*, 57 (1), 1–22. doi:10.17763/haer.57.1.j463w79r56455411.

Shulman, L. (2005). Signature Pedagogies in the Professions. *Daedalus*, 134(3), 52–9. doi:10.1162/0011526054622015.

Shulman, L. (2015). PCK: Its Genesis and Exodus. In A. K. Berry, P. Friedrichsen, and J. J. Loughran (Eds), *Re-examining Pedagogical Content Knowledge in Science Education* (3–13). New York: Routledge.

Sides, J., Tesler, M., and Vavreck, L. (2018). *Identity Crisis.* Princeton, NJ: Princeton University Press.

Skourdoumbis, A. (2017). Assessing the Productivity of Schools through Two 'What Works' Inputs, Teacher Quality, and Teacher Effectiveness. *Educational Research for Policy and Practice*, 16(3), 205–17. doi:10.1007/s10671-016-9210-y.

Sleeter, C. (2001). Preparing Teachers for Culturally Diverse Schools: Research and the Overwhelming Presence of Whiteness. *Journal of Teacher Education*, 55(2), 94–106. doi:10.1177/00224 87101052002002.

Sleeter, C. (2017). Critical Race Theory and the Whiteness of Teacher Education. *Urban Education*, 52(2), 155–69. doi:10.1177/0042085916668957.

Smagorinsky, P., Lakly, A., and Johnson, T. H. (2002). Acquiescence, Accommodation, and Resistance in Learning to Teach within a Prescribed Curriculum. *English Education*, 34, 187–213. Available at http://www.jstor.org/stable/40173127. Accessed 22 October 2022.

Smagorinsky, P., Cook, L. S., Jackson, A. Y., Moore, C., and Fry, P. G. (2004). Tensions in Learning to Teach: Accommodation and the Development of a Teaching Identity. *Journal of Teacher Education*, 55, 8–24. doi:10.1177/0022487103260067.

Smith, K., and Flores, M. A. (2019). The Janus Faced Teacher Educator. *European Journal of Teacher Education*, 42(4), 433–46. doi:10.1080/02619768.2019.1646242.

Souto-Manning, M. (2019). Toward Praxically-Just Transformations: Interrupting Racism in Teacher Education. *Journal of Education for Teaching*, 45(1), 97–113. doi:10.1080/02607476.2019.1550608.

Springbett, O. (2018). The Professional Identities of Teacher Educators in Three Further Education Colleges: An Entanglement of Discourse and Practice. *Journal of Education for Teaching*, 44(2), 149–61. doi:10.1080/02607476.2017.1370481.

Steadman, S. (2018). Defining Practice: Exploring the Meaning of Practice in the Process of Learning to Teach. *TEAN Journal*, 10(1), 3–9.

Steadman, S. (2020). The Making of Teachers: A Study of Trainee Teachers' Experiences of Learning to Teach in Different Postgraduate Routes in England. Unpublished PhD thesis, King's College London.

Steadman, S. (2021). Conflict, Transition and Agency: Reconceptualising the Process of Learning to Teach. *Teaching and Teacher Education*, 107, 1–12. doi:10.1016/j.tate.2021.103475.

Steadman, S., and Ellis, V. (2021). Teaching Quality, Social Mobility and 'Opportunity' in England: The Case of the Teaching and Leadership Innovation Fund. *European Journal of Teacher Education*, 44(3), 399–414. doi:10.1080/02619768.2021.1901078.

Swennen, A., Jones, K., and Volman, M. (2010). Teacher Educators: Their Identities, Sub-identities and Implications for Professional Development. *Professional Development in Education*, 36(1–2), 131–48. doi:10.1080/19415250903457893.

Tajfel, H., and Turner, J. C. (1979). An Integrative Theory of Intergroup Conflict. *The Social Psychology of Intergroup Relations*, 33(47), 74.

Taylor, C. (1977). What Is Human Agency? In T. Mischel (Ed.), *The Self: Psychological and Philosophical Issues*. Oxford: Oxford University Press.

Taylor, W. (1983). Teacher Education: Achievements, Shortcomings and Perspectives. Paper presented at The John Adams Memorial Lecture, The Institute of Education, London.

TEMAG. (2014). *Action Now: Classroom Ready Teachers*. Canberra: AITSL. Available at https://www.education.gov.au/teaching-and-school-leadership/resources/action-now-classr oom-ready-teachers-report-0. Accessed 22 October 2022.

Tereshchenko, A., Mills, M., and Bradbury, A. (2020). *Making Progress? Employment and Retention of BAME Teachers in England*. London: UCL Institute of Education.

Thornton, K. (2014). Mentors as Educational Leaders and Change Agents. *International Journal of Mentoring and Coaching in Education*, 3(1), 18–31. doi:10.1108/IJMCE-07-2013-0038.

Thurston, D. (2010). The Invisible Educators: Exploring the Development of Teacher Educators in the Further Education System. *Teaching in Lifelong Learning*, 2(1), 47–55. doi:10.5920/till.2010.2147.

Timoštšuk, I., and Ugaste, A. (2012). The Role of Emotions in Student Teachers' Professional Identity. *European Journal of Teacher Education*, 35(4), 421–33. doi:10.1080/02619768.2012.662637.

Toom, A., Pyhältö, K., and Rust, F. (2015). Teachers' Professional Agency in Contradictory Times. *Teachers and Teaching*, 21(6), 615–23. doi:10.1080/13540602.2015.1044334.

Torrance, H. (2018). Blaming the Victim: Assessment, Examinations, and the Responsibilisation of Students and Teachers in Neo-liberal Governance. In C. Halse, C. Hartung, and J. Wright (Eds), *Responsibility and Responsibilisation in Education* (83–97). London: Routledge.

Tryggvason, M. T. (2012). Perceptions of Identity among Finnish University-Based Subject Teacher Educators. *European Journal of Teacher Education*, 35(3), 289–303. doi:10.1080/02619768.201 1.633998.

Turner, J. C., Hogg, M. A., Oakes, P. J., Reicher, S. D., and Wetherell, M. S. (1987). *Rediscovering the Social Group: A Self-Categorization Theory*. Cambridge, MA: Blackwell.

Turnuklu, E. B., and Yesildere, S. (2007). The Pedagogical Content Knowledge in Mathematics: Preservice Primary Mathematics Teachers' Perspectives in Turkey. *Issues in the Undergraduate Mathematics Preparation of School Teachers*, 1, 1–13.

Uibu, K., Salo, A., Ugaste, A., and Rasku-Puttonen, H. (2017). Beliefs about Teaching Held by Student Teachers and School-Based Teacher Educators. *Teaching and Teacher Education*, 63, 396–404. doi:10.1016/j.tate.2017.01.016.

UCET. (2020). UCET Intellectual Base of Teacher Education Report. Available at https://www.ucet.ac.uk/11675/intellectual-base-of-teacher-education-report-updated-february-2020. Accessed 22 October 2022.

Urrieta, L. (2007). Identity Production in Figured Worlds: How Some Mexican Americans Become Chicana/o Activist Educators. *The Urban Review*, 39(2), 117–44. doi:10.1007/s11256-007-0050-11.

van Dick, R., and Haslam, S. A. (2012). Stress and Well-Being in the Workplace: Support for Key Propositions from the Social Identity Approach. In J. Jetten, C. Haslam, and S. A. Haslam (Eds), *The Social Cure: Identity, Health, and Well-Being* (175–194). Hove: Psychology Press.

Vasilyuk, F. (1988). *The Psychology of Experiencing*. Moscow: Progress.

Vavrus, M. (2010). Critical Multiculturalism and Higher Education: Resistance and Possibilities within Teacher Education. In S. May and C. Sleeter (Eds), *Critical Multiculturalism – Theory and Praxis* (19–31). New York: Routledge.

Veenman, S. (1984). Perceived Problems of Beginning Teachers. *Review of Educational Research*, 54(2), 143–78. doi:10.3102/00346543054002143.

Vygotsky, L. (1978). *Mind in Society*. Cambridge, MA: Harvard University Press.

Vygotsky, L. S. (1994). The Problem of the Environment. In R. Van der Veer and J. Jaan Valsine (Eds), *The Vygotsky Reader* (338–54). Oxford: Wiley-Blackwell.

Waitoller, F. R., and Kozleski, E. B. (2013). Understanding and Dismantling Barriers for Partnerships for Inclusive Education: A Cultural Historical Activity Theory Perspective. *International Journal of Whole Schooling*, 9(1), 23–42.

Warin, J., and Muldoon, J. (2009). Wanting to Be 'Known': Redefining Self-Awareness through an Understanding of Self-Narration Processes in Educational Transitions. *British Educational Research Journal*, 35(2), 289–303. doi:10.1080/01411920802043000.

Warin, J., Maddock, M., Pell, A., and Hargreaves, L. (2006).
Resolving Identity Dissonance through Reflective and Reflexive
Practice in Teaching. *Reflective Practice*, 7(2), 231–43.
doi:10.1080/14623940600688670.

Watt, H., Richardson, P., and Tysvaer, N. (2007). Profiles
of Beginning Teachers' Professional Engagement and
Career Development Aspirations. In A. Berry, A. Clemans,
and A. Kostogriz (Eds), *Dimensions of Professional
Learning: Professionalism, Practice and Identity* (155–75).
Boston: Sense Publishers.

Weber, S. J., and Mitchell, C. A. (1995). *That's Funny You Don't
Look like a Teacher! Interrogating Images, Identity, and Popular
Culture*. London: Falmer Press.

Wenger, E. (2000). Communities of Practice and Social Learning
Systems. *Organization*, 7, 225–46. doi:10.1177/135050840072002.

Wenger, E. (1998). *Communities of Practice: Learning, Meaning and
Identity*. New York: Cambridge University Press.

White, E. (2013). Exploring the Professional Development Needs of
New Teacher Educators Situated Solely in School: Pedagogical
Knowledge and Professional Identity. *Professional Development
in Education*, 39(1), 82–98. doi:10.1080/19415257.2012.708667.

White, S. (2019). Teacher Educators for New Times? Redefining
an Important Occupational Group. *Journal of Education for
Teaching*, 45(2), 200–13. doi:10.1080/02607476.2018.1548174.

Widodo, H., and Allamnakhrah, A. (2020). The Impact of a Blended
Professional Learning Community on Teacher Educators'
Professional Identity: Towards Sustainable Teacher Professional
Development. *Journal of Education for Teaching*, 46(3), 408–10.
doi:10.1080/02607476.2020.1761249.

Williams, J. (2013). Boundary Crossing and Working in the Third
Space: Implications for a Teacher Educator's Identity and
Practice. *Studying Teacher Education*, 9(2), 118–29. doi:10.1080/
17425964.2013.808046.

Williams, J., and Ritter, J. K. (2010). Constructing New Professional
Identities through Self-Study: From Teacher to Teacher Educator.
Professional Development in Education, 36(1–2), 77–92.
doi:10.1080/19415250903454833.

Williams, J., Ritter, J., and Bullock, S. M. (2012). Understanding
the Complexity of Becoming a Teacher Educator: Experience,
Belonging, and Practice within a Professional Learning

Community. *Studying Teacher Education*, 8(3), 245–60. doi:10.1080/17425964.2012.719130.

Williams, R. (1976). *Keywords – A Vocabulary of Culture and Society*. London: Fontana.

Yendol-Hoppey, D., and Franco, Y. (2014). In Search of Signature Pedagogy for PDS Teacher Education: A Review of Articles Published in 'School-University Partnerships'. *School-University Partnerships*, 7(1), 17–34.

Zeichner, K. (1999). The New Scholarship in Teacher Education. *Educational Researcher*, 28(9), 4–15. doi:10.3102/0013189X028009004.

Zeichner, K. (2005). Becoming a Teacher Educator: A Personal Perspective. *Teaching and Teacher Education*, 21(2), 117–24. doi:10.1016/j.tate.2004.12.001.

Zeichner, K. (2007). Accumulating Knowledge across Self-Studies in Teacher Education. *Journal of Teacher Education*, 58(1), 36–46. doi:10.1177/0022487106296219.

Zeichner, K. (2012). The Turn Once Again toward Practice-Based Teacher Education. *Journal of Teacher Education*, 63(5), 376–82. doi:10.1177/0022487112445789.

Zeichner, K. (2015). Engaging Local Communities in the Preparation of Teachers. *Kappa Delta Pi Record*, 51(3), 118–20. doi:10.1080/00228958.2015.1056662.

Zeichner, K., and Tabachnik, B. R. (1981). Are the Effects of University Teacher Education 'Washed Out' by School Experience? *Journal of Teacher Education*, 32(3). doi:10.1177/002248718103200302.

Zeichner, K., and Bier, M. (2015). Opportunities and Pitfalls in the Turn Towards Clinical Experience in US Teacher Education. In E. R. Hollins (Ed.), *Rethinking Field Experiences in Preservice Teacher Preparation: Meeting New Challenges for Accountability* (20–46). New York: Routledge.

Zeichner, K., Payne, K. A., and Brayko, K. (2015). Democratizing Teacher Education. *Journal of Teacher Education*, 66(2), 122–35. doi:10.1177/0022487114560908.

Zeichner, K., Bowman M., Guillen, L., and Napolitan, K. (2016). Engaging and Working in Solidarity with Local Communities in Preparing the Teachers of Their Children. *Journal of Teacher Education*, 67(4), 1–14. doi:10.1177/0022487116660623.

INDEX